UNSCRIPTED

SHARING
THE GOSPEL
AS LIFE
HAPPENS

UNSCRIPTED

SHARING
THE GOSPEL
AS LIFE
HAPPENS

JEFF IORG

NEW HOPE
PUBLISHERS
Gospel-Centered. Missions-Driven.

BIRMINGHAM, ALABAMA

New Hope® Publishers
PO Box 12065
Birmingham, AL 35202-2065
NewHopeDigital.com
New Hope Publishers is a division of WMU®.

Library of Congress has cataloged an earlier edition as follows:

Iorg, Jeff.
   Live like a missionary : giving your life for what matters most / Jeff Iorg.
      p. cm.
   ISBN 978-1-59669-305-0 (sc)
1. Witness bearing (Christianity) 2.   Christian life—Baptist authors.
I. Title.
   BV4520.I67 2011
   248'.5—dc23

                         2011016853

ISBN-10: 1-59669-408-4
ISBN-13: 978-1-59669-408-8

Designers: Cover: Michel Lê
Interior: Kay Bishop

N144114 • 0514 • 3M1

DEDICATION

One of the best things about getting older is living long enough to have old friends.

This book is dedicated to Keith and Jane, Gary and Susan, Bobby and Gwen, Larry and Jean, Rick and Suzanne, and Rusty and Sheila. All of you are everyday Christians who have changed your communities and the world by living out the message of this book.

You inspire me.
Thanks for being my friends.

TABLE OF CONTENTS

LIFE HAPPENS—
NO SCRIPT PROVIDED

CHAPTER 1

CONVERSATIONS ABOUT THE GOSPEL

ANN SAT DOWN ON THE BUS BESIDE a young woman dressed in black, all tatted up, with a pentagram necklace on a choker chain. Since Ann is one of those people others find easy to talk with, it wasn't long before she learned her new friend was a lesbian, gothic, witch. Sidestepping the lesbian and gothic issues, Ann asked her to describe what it meant to be a witch. After hearing her explanation of Wiccan religion, Ann responded by telling her story of following Jesus. How did she know what to say? There aren't any specialized seminars on sharing the gospel with lesbian, gothic, witches. Ann engaged her seatmate in a conversation, tailoring the gospel to meet the needs of some-one obviously searching for personal identity and meaning in life. She talked about Jesus with a lesbian, gothic, witch.

There's no script for conversations like that.

Janet had an acquaintance, Cheryl, who lived across the street. Like many neighbors today, they waved from their cars as they drove away or spoke briefly if they were both working in their yards on the same day. Cheryl gave birth to twins, so Janet took her a small gift and wished her well. Their relationship developed a little more through that act of kindness, but not that much, since the twins kept Cheryl busy. These two younger moms didn't spend much time together for several months. Then, tragically, Cheryl's husband was killed in a work-related accident. She was left a 20-something widow with twin toddlers. Janet later told me, "I didn't know what to say or do. But I knew I had to do something. So, I baked a casserole and took it over. When Cheryl answered the door, I said, 'I am so sorry for what's happened. I don't know what to say. But I care about you and I'll do anything I can to help you.'"

Even though she didn't know what to say—who would?—she risked speaking up, saying *something*, initiating a conversation to communicate compassion. A casserole started a conversation which led to talking about Jesus.

Unscripted, yet so simple.

And ultimately effective, as the conversation continued over the next six months culminating in Cheryl's confession of Jesus as Lord and Savior—followed by her baptism at our church.

Larry had read more than 200 books on New Age religion. His company had a corporate chaplain, but Larry usually ignored him since his beliefs were askance from the chaplain's orthodox Christianity. Then Larry starting reading the Bible. After a few months, he asked the chaplain if they could get together—in Larry's words—"so I can ask some questions about religion." The chaplain expected some esoteric questions based on the voluminous religious reading he knew Larry had done. When they met, Larry's first question was, "What does it mean to be born again and is that anything like having your sins forgiven?" Hello! That wasn't what he expected to hear. Forty minutes later, after the chaplain answered a string of insightful questions about the gospel, Larry committed himself to Jesus.

Unscripted, answering unexpected questions about Jesus.

Todd was sitting in his cubicle reading an obscure book about metaphysics and religious faith. When asked by a friend why he was reading that particular book, he replied, "I'm looking for truth. Truth, man, that's all I want to find." His friend told him about another book that was about truth, and asked if he would read it if he gave it to him as a gift. When Todd agreed he would, the friend gave him a popular book on why it's reasonable to believe in God. That conversation is ongoing.

Definitely, unscripted. But, hopefully soon, they will be talking about Jesus.

CONVERSATIONS, NOT LECTURES

These are stories of personal evangelism—conversations about Jesus as life happens, in the ebb and flow of birth, death, work, and trips on the bus. At least that's what personal evangelism is supposed to look like. Unfortunately, evangelism has a troubled image these days. It's become a dirty word for Christians and non-Christians alike. Unbelievers disdain evangelism—often equating it with dogmatic legalists winning heavy-handed, judgmental, presumptuous, religious arguments. Being evangelized means being lectured— harangued really—in distasteful ways for everyone involved. At least that's the popular, media-driven perspective.

While most Christians don't think of evangelism that negatively, they still perceive personal evangelism as an onerous, uncomfortable task to be avoided at all costs. They tolerate guilt-inducing sermons on the subject, and may even feel some wistful longing to be more effective in telling others about Jesus, but rarely do anything about it. When they do muster the courage to try to witness to someone, they feel inadequate—spiritually and intellectually—often stammering through what they think they are supposed to say, rather than sharing honestly from the heart. They wrongly think sharing Jesus is delivering a canned spiel or sales pitch.

How sad!

The word *evangel* means "herald of good news." An evangelist, therefore, is supposed to be a "good news teller." Personal evangelism should be about "telling someone good news." Simply put— it's talking about Jesus! What happened? When did so much good news become bad news? How did such a positive concept—the privilege of reporting the best news of all (the death, burial, and resurrection of Jesus with a personal invitation to follow Him)— turn into such a distasteful experience? More importantly, if you have succumbed to such negative thinking, what can be done to change your image of personal evangelism? How can you develop a healthier perspective on sharing the good news of Jesus? How can you rediscover conversing about Jesus—as a normal part of life—as the essence of sharing the gospel?

Effective personal evangelism isn't about memorizing answers to complicated religious questions, winning arguments with religious intellectuals, or convincing people to do something they really don't want to do. Evangelism is about connecting people to Jesus and connecting Jesus with your community—spontaneously, joyfully, and honestly. It's not drudgery, some bitter religious medicine you have to stomach occasionally to absolve false guilt for not being more open about your faith. The joy of personal evangelism needs to be recaptured by believers as characteristic of our highest privilege—sharing the good news of Jesus with people we care about. We've got to rediscover what it means to talk with people about Jesus—conversationally, rationally, and sometimes incrementally over long periods of time—until we have successfully communicated the gospel. Personal evangelism is supposed to be like that—unscripted—engaging people where they are, as they come, authentically connecting them with the gospel. That's what this book is about!

WHOSE RESPONSIBILITY IS THIS?

If you have read this far, you have some interest in or sense of responsibility for sharing the gospel. Otherwise, why would this book interest you? A legitimate question is, Are you really responsible to share the gospel with other people? If so, when did you become responsible for doing so? When did you become responsible for telling people about Jesus?

The answer may surprise you. It happened at the moment of your conversion—and it happened to every believer (not just people like pastors or missionaries or verbal extroverts who really like to talk). Paul wrote, "I was made servant of this gospel by the gift of God's grace that was given to me by the working of His power" (Ephesians 3:7). He traced his responsibility to serve the gospel to his conversion. Serving the gospel is an interesting concept. How can you serve the gospel? What's the one thing the gospel, which is inherently powerful, can't do for itself? The answer—share itself. The gospel has been committed to people like you and me. Believers are

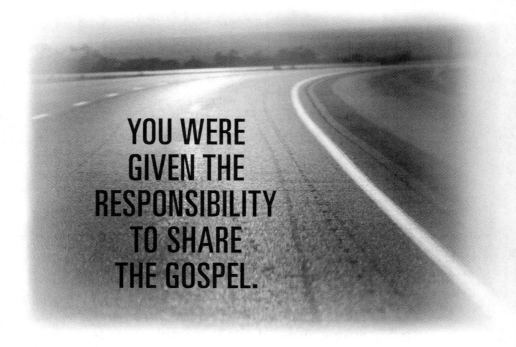

YOU WERE GIVEN THE RESPONSIBILITY TO SHARE THE GOSPEL.

responsible to serve the gospel by doing the only thing the gospel can't do for itself—sharing it with unbelievers.

Paul was a well-known missionary in the first century. His call to be a missionary (to go to new places with the gospel) was a subsequent experience (Acts 13:1–3) separate from his conversion (Acts 9:1–19). These were two distinct events. While you may not have had the second experience (being called to be a missionary), if you are a Christian, the first one (becoming a servant of the gospel) definitely happened to you. When you received Jesus as your Lord and Savior—when you received "the gift of God's grace that was given to (you) by the working of His power"—you became responsible to "proclaim . . . the incalculable riches of the Messiah" (Ephesians 3:8).

You may not have realized you were given this responsibility at your conversion, but that doesn't mean it didn't happen. You may have committed your life to Jesus as a young person, praying at Vacation Bible School for Jesus to save you. Perhaps you came to Jesus later in life—after years of rebellion against God. You may have trusted Jesus as your Savior and Lord without much biblical background or after years of study. No matter how or when you became a Christian, in the moment of your conversion you were given the responsibility to share the gospel with other people.

You may be surprised such a heavy responsibility was given to you, without you even knowing it. Don't be alarmed. Getting more than you bargained for when you make a commitment happens all the time. For example, students go to college and declare a major. Sometime later they enroll in courses based on their degree program's requirements. Then, when they finally receive the class assignments, they are astonished at the workload. Students have coined a name for it: "syllabus shock." It's that sinking feeling they get when they know they must do more than they bargained for with no alternative except bearing down and fulfilling their newfound obligations.

The most common illustration of this process, however, is marriage. A young couple stands before a pastor and pledges their devotion. They are sure of their love and confident they fully understand the privileges and responsibilities of marriage. Riiight! It's usually only a few days, never more than a few weeks, before a couple begins to understand marriage entails much more than they anticipated. When a couple says, "I do," they really have very little idea what they are doing. Once again a commitment has been made without understanding the totality of its implications and obligations.

I often joke with my wife, Ann, that I have been married to three different women. We have been married for more than 30 years, and Ann has changed significantly in those three decades. On the other hand, of course, I am the same sweet, wonderful man she first married! Once, I teased, "Ann, I have been married to three different women. First, there was New Wife Ann. Then there was Supermom Ann. Now, you have morphed into Ministry Dynamo Ann. How many more of you are there?" She smiled, "I'm not sure. Probably at least two . . . just to keep it interesting." Interesting, indeed! Our initial commitment only created the framework for discovering the serendipities of our relationship. We had no idea all that was entailed when we exchanged our wedding vows.

So it is in your relationship with Jesus. In the moment of your conversion, you were saved. Your sins were forgiven and you received the gift of eternal life (John 3:16). Those results were desired and anticipated. But so much more happened! You were baptized by the Holy Spirit and experienced your initial filling by the Spirit (1 Corinthians 12:13). You were given spiritual gifts

(1 Corinthians 12; Romans 12:3–8; Ephesians 4:11–12). You were sealed by the Spirit (Ephesians 1:13) and made a member of the global church (Ephesians 3:10–12). You became part of the body of Christ, with certain functions assigned pertinent to your gifting, background, and experiences (1 Corinthians 12:12–27). If you were a teenager converted at youth camp, all you thought happened when you prayed at the bonfire service was you were saved from your sins. But that was only one aspect of the myriad, mystical changes God accomplished in you that night. So much else happened, including your assignment to share the gospel with family, friends, and other people God brings into your life.

IT'S ABOUT PEOPLE, NOT PLACES

One of the most commonly misunderstood insights from Paul's testimony relates to the objective of his evangelistic activities. Believers often equate sharing the gospel with going somewhere to connect with strangers. Whether it's door-to-door cold-calling or a missions trip to another country, we often think the "out there" people are those we should prioritize reaching with the gospel. Strangers you haven't met and people in distant lands do need the gospel. But for most believers, their best personal evangelism is with people they already know and they are uniquely suited to reach. Your conversations about Jesus are most likely to happen as life happens right around you.

Paul wrote, "This grace was given to me . . . to proclaim to the Gentiles" (Ephesians 3:8). He further underscored Gentiles as his evangelistic objective when he wrote, "I have written to you more boldly on some points because of the grace given me by God to be a minister of Christ Jesus to the Gentiles, serving as a priest of God's good news" (Romans 15:15–16). Paul identified the Gentiles as the people he was uniquely suited for and responsible to reach.

When you share the gospel, you choose a group of people as the object of your outreach and strategically invest yourself in communicating the gospel to them. Paul was committed to reaching Gentiles. Admittedly, that's a large people group. Yours will most likely be much smaller—like the teenagers at your high school, the mothers in your child's play group, the men who work the night shift with you, or the guys you play basketball with twice a week.

For about 20 years, while serving as a pastor and denominational executive, my personal missions field was families in community youth sports programs. Since our three children were all athletes, this was a natural connection for our family. More than just showing up for the games, we developed meaningful friendships and strategically reached out to sports families like ours. We saw several people commit themselves to Jesus. Now, even though my children are adults, my Gentiles are still people in the baseball community in our area. My love for the game, my understanding of "baseball people" (yes, they are like a tribe all their own), and my comfort level engaging them with the gospel has made this a fertile field for the gospel.

Your evangelism assignment, and you have one if you are a follower of Jesus, is to reach people with the gospel. So, the question becomes, Which people? To put it in Pauline terms, Who are your Gentiles? Who are the people God has uniquely equipped you to reach? What people group is your responsibility? You are called to reach people in your community—people you live and work among on a regular basis. And, if you sense a call to go outside your

WHO ARE
YOUR GENTILES?

community (like going on a missions trip or becoming a missionary), before you travel around the world to work with Sudanese refugees, for example, why not work with those already relocated in your area? Test your call to a people outside your cultural (and perhaps linguistic or geographic boundaries) by first finding similar people in your area and investing yourself in them. Remember, if you won't drive across town to witness to Russians, why should a church or mission board fund your deployment to Moscow?

If you are burdened for orphans in Rwanda, test your call by working with orphans in your community. If you feel you should reach out to the poor in Mexico, first find recent immigrants in your area and invest yourself with them. If God wants you to share the gospel with unwed mothers in a Spanish prison, first volunteer in your local woman's prison. If you want to care for AIDS victims in Africa, first connect with your local AIDS hospice and offer your services.

No matter the people group you desire to serve—orphans, immigrants, prisoners, or outcasts—you can find them in your community. No matter the nationality you long to connect with, you can find people from almost every country in every major city. If God is leading you to reach a specific people outside your immediate experience, get busy! Don't assume prior cultural adaptation, linguistic preparation, or geographic relocation must precede obedience. It usually works in the reverse order. Obey God now, doing what you can where you are, and trust Him to call you across the nation or around the world as a result of your passionate outreach, not to validate it.

In the meantime, focus on sharing the gospel where you are, with the people you know, or with those in your community you are intentionally trying to reach. While some are called to go out of their way to share the gospel with new people in new places, the focus of this book is sharing the gospel with the people you already know—the missions field all around you.

CHANGING YOUR IMAGE OF EVANGELISM
Even once you understand your responsibility to share the gospel, it may still be difficult to envision yourself as a personal evangelist.

Your perspective may be skewed, making it hard to picture yourself in that role. You need help reimagining personal evangelism so you will feel comfortable doing it.

The Bible uses several images to describe evangelists, and none of them involves slicked-back hair or ugly plaid sports coats! They don't include used car sales techniques or pushy telemarketer-type memorized scripts. Biblical images communicate different aspects of what it means to connect people to Jesus. The emphasis, however, is authentic relationships—people connecting with people. The images are all tweaked to make them relational in their application, consistently reinforcing the theme that personal evangelism is about relationships. It's about connecting family and friends, work associates and community members, and even the occasional stranger you befriend to Jesus. Evangelizing is about building relationships, creating networks, and constructing conversational bridges by which the gospel can pass from person to person. As an evangelist, you're a nonverbal as well as verbal connecter—linking Jesus with your friends and family, sharing the gospel through relational channels. Evangelism is connecting people to Jesus; connecting the gospel to your community. If *evangelist* is still too pejorative in your mind, think of yourself of as a connecter—a conversationalist who brings people together with Jesus through meaningful dialogue about the gospel.

To further reshape your image of personal evangelism, consider some of the following biblical images for evangelism. As already stated, these images are all relational—taking common human activities and filling them with new spiritual meaning. And always, that meaning involves connecting people with God and His gospel. In all these images, there's an adventurous unpredictability because life is unscripted. Here are half a dozen of these relationally potent comparisons to get you started on the reimaging process.

Evangelists are like fishermen. Jesus met with a group of disciples working as commercial fishermen. They had fished all night, without any luck. Jesus told them to try a new part of the lake. Dozens of fish filled their nets! Jesus used this object lesson to challenge the men to become evangelists. He told them, "From now on you will be catching people!" (Luke 5:10). Commercial fishing, in those days as today, involves casting a large net over a potential catch and gathering the fish for processing. Evangelists are like fishermen, they cast the gospel widely trusting Jesus will draw those to Himself who are part of his catch. Fishermen are also hard workers, who must ply their trade day after day. Fresh fish are the only kind of fish most people want to buy. Evangelists work hard, day by day, committed to sharing the gospel through life's normal ebb and flow. They know connecting people to Jesus takes time, persistent effort, and steady patience. Fishing for people really is a lot like catching fish.

Evangelists are like farmers. Jesus taught a large crowd of people about reaching people using the parable of a farmer (Mark 4:1–20). He described a sower who went through his field casting seed on various types of soil—good ground, a packed path, rocky scrabble, thorny bramble. Some seeds, in the best soil, thrived and produced a multifold increase. The other soils, not much, if any results. Jesus explained the parable this way. The farmer's seed represented the Word of God. The soils symbolized the readiness of the hearers—who respond in various ways at different levels of commitment. The good soil represented the person who was ready and able to receive the gospel, enjoying its fullness in producing remarkable life change. Like the fisherman, the farmer-evangelist broadcasts the gospel to many expecting a significant response. But the farmer image has another important point—not everyone you try to connect to the gospel is ready to connect. Responses vary, but that's not your concern. Cast gospel seed far and wide, know it will receive a mixed response—but also trusting at least some people will respond positively.

Evangelists are like witnesses. Jesus' followers had recently watched Him go through a public trial. They had abandoned him during the worst of it, even Peter profanely denying he knew Jesus. A few weeks later, just before He left earth the final time, Jesus told His followers, "You will be my witnesses in Jerusalem, in all Judea and Samaria, and to the ends of the earth" (Acts 1:8). A witness is a person who tells the truth about what they have heard, seen, or experienced. With their recent failure during Jesus' judicial process still fresh in their minds, Jesus used the analogy of being a trial witness to describe their future responsibility to him. As an evangelist, you don't have to invent the message you are supposed to deliver. The gospel—the good news about Jesus—is your message. Your role is reporting your gospel experience to other people—telling what has happened to you. There's no argument against a changed life. Witnesses tell what they have seen and heard, what they have experienced, and how others can be similarly impacted by connecting to Jesus.

Evangelists are like searchers. Some of the most selfless and gallant people work in search and rescue operations, helping distressed people find safety. They plunge into raging oceans, scale snow-covered peaks, and otherwise risk their lives for the good of others. Jesus used searching, and described various types of searchers, as models of evangelism. For example, Jesus told parables about a shepherd searching for a lost sheep (Luke 15:1–7) and a woman searching for a lost coin (Luke 15:8–10). He told another parable about a man who gave a large banquet—but no guests came. He then sent his servant to retrieve the "poor, maimed, blind, and lame" (Luke 14:21) as well as compelling others to come from "the highways and lanes . . . so that my house may be filled" (Luke 14:23). Connecting people to Jesus and connecting the gospel to your community requires focused effort. Diligence, initiative, and old-fashioned hard work are part of evangelizing others. Implicit in the meaning of these parables is the value of what has been lost. More than sheep, coins, or anonymous banquet guests—people you know and love are lost without a relationship to God through Jesus. They must be found! Personal evangelists are driven to get this done, finding creative ways to build bridges to people who are far from God.

Evangelists are like parents. While no parents are perfect, most do the best they can loving and nurturing their children. They want the best for them and make countless sacrifices—large and small—to make sure (as more than one parent has said) "my kids have a better life than I had." That's a common theme for many parents. Paul, writing of his experience in launching the Corinthian church, reminded his followers he was "their father in the gospel" (1 Corinthians 4:15). Fathers (and mothers too) have a continuing responsibility to shape their children toward the most positive life possible. Parents have to put up with all kinds of challenges—

from school to relationships to puberty to finances—while guiding their children toward maturity. Evangelists are often like parents in relating to their closest family and friends about the gospel. Sharing Jesus takes place in the context of a continuing relationship. You can't just "speak your piece" and move on. Family and friends are still there the next day. This image of evangelism is important for ongoing relationships. You, in a sense, parent people in the gospel and toward Jesus. You steadily speak and model the gospel—not just share it once and hope for the best. Evangelists realize gospel-connections, at least some, can take years and patiently, like good parents, hang in there until the job is finished.

Evangelists are like ambassadors. While you may be able to see yourself as a farmer or fisherman, searcher, or even a parent or witness, it may be tougher to imagine yourself as an ambassador. Yet, the Bible says we are "ambassadors for Christ" (1 Corinthians 5:20) bearing the "message of reconciliation" (1 Corinthians 5:19) God has committed to us. An ambassador is a person who represents a head of state to the senior leaders of another nation. For the United States, ambassadors represent the President. The ambassador represents our government and all it stands for embodied in a personal presence in a foreign, sometimes hostile, environment. In an age of instant communication, this role may seem less significant than it was in the past. But think about how ambassadors functioned throughout history. When an ambassador traveled internationally, he was on his own representing his country without frequent communication to guide his decision making. He had to know his ruler well and understand the core assignment he had been given. An ambassador is a significant leader—a person with authority to represent senior leaders and make world-changing decisions. This image adds to the stature and status of evangelists. You represent God. You are in foreign, perhaps hostile territory. You have His authority to act and His message (the gospel) to deliver. Ambassadors have the privilege of representing the God of the universe to people. What could be more lofty and noble than that?

As you reimage personal evangelism, which of these images is most meaningful to you? Which helps change your view of being an evangelist? As a new picture comes into focus, see yourself in the center of it—talking about the gospel during unscripted conversations with people who share life with you. That's a very healthy image of personal evangelism.

TWO CONVICTIONS—THEN LET'S GET STARTED

This book is based on two convictions. First, every believer is responsible to share the gospel. We have nailed that down in this chapter. Second, every believer can learn to share the gospel more effectively. That's the focus of the rest of the book.

No Christian is exempt from these two convictions. You might assume my being a seminary president—teaching others to do ministry and administrating a faculty and staff for the same purpose—fulfills my responsibility for serving the gospel. It doesn't. Working in this role helps others accelerate the fulfillment of the Great Commission, but it doesn't satisfy my personal responsibility. So, almost every week, I devote time to evangelizing young men in the professional baseball community. It's not glamorous work. It's making friends with players, listening to their struggles, responding to their personal crises, putting up with the callousness of some toward God and His Word, tolerating spiritual immaturity, patiently answering their questions, praying for them and with them—all while sitting in a dugout or an equipment room, often while they eat lunch with a Bible balanced on one knee. It's hard, sometimes frustrating work. But the eternal rewards are well worth the effort!

As you become more intentional about sharing the gospel, and see the results, you will reap the same rewards—people you care about enjoying a new quality of life now and eternal life forever.

WHAT COMES FIRST?

Are you ready to share to gospel more effectively? If so, what should you do first? Great question! The foundations for effective personal evangelism are spiritual truth and spiritual disciplines—not sales techniques or memorized answers to obscure theological questions.

Let's start by learning to pray more effectively in relation to personal evangelism. Before you go to others, go to God first. There's no substitute for prayer before, during, and after evangelistic encounters. Kneeling precedes going, praying precedes doing.

Shallow praying won't win the spiritual battle inherent with sharing the gospel. Fortunately, the Bible has specific instructions about how to pray, as well as examples of praying related specifically to personal evangelism. Let's shape our praying toward those ends as we move into the next chapter.

SPIRITUAL FOUNDATIONS FOR SHARING THE GOSPEL AS LIFE HAPPENS

CHAPTER 2

PRAYING FIRST, PRAYING OFTEN

THERE IS A DIFFERENCE BETWEEN presuming and assuming—but neither is very helpful when it comes to prayer. When we presume, we operate as if something has happened—when it may not have happened. When we assume, we take responsibility for making something happen. We must not presume God will work through us apart from prayer or assume someone else will do our praying. Each of us must take responsibility for praying strategically and specifically for effectiveness in sharing the gospel. Fervent prayer is essential for personal evangelism. Since life is unscripted—you never know what a day will bring—you have to pray much and often for God's guidance and power for witnessing.

This has been a hard lesson for me. I'm too self-sufficient for my own good. Writing about prayer is like me teaching a golf lesson. My skill level, described in golf jargon as a hacker, means I'm acquainted with the game but not qualified to teach it. I feel the same way about prayer. I pray, but I always feel inadequate in this area. I'm not a prayer warrior or great intercessor. Thankfully, you don't have to depend on my insights or example (or anyone else's for that matter) to learn how to pray related to evangelizing others. The Bible has clear instructions and timeless examples to help us in this important area.

When you pray about sharing your faith, you want to pray in a way you can be sure God hears and answers. Is this possible? Absolutely. The Bible says:

> *Now this is the confidence we have before Him: whenever we ask anything according to His will, He hears us. And if we know that He hears whatever we ask, we know that we have what we have asked Him for* (1 JOHN 5:14–15).

The key to powerful prayer is praying according to God's will. The simplest and surest way to pray according to God's will is to pray biblical prayers. If instructions to pray, requests for prayer, or actual prayers are found in the Bible, you can be sure they pass the "God's will" test. When you base your praying on the following models, you can be confident God hears and answers. There's no subject more important to God than reaching the lost. He wants unbelievers to become believers, so much He sent Jesus to redeem them and left us here to tell them about Jesus. People being converted are definitely God's will. The New Testament has five specific prayer requests, instructions about prayer, and transcribed prayers modeling how to pray related to evangelism. Let's look at these examples as we develop greater capacity to pray according to God's will on the crucial issue of leading the lost to Jesus.

PRAY FOR MORE PEOPLE TO JOIN THE HARVEST

Jesus told us to pray for more people to join His harvest. The Bible says:

> *Then Jesus went to all the towns and villages, teaching in their synagogues, preaching the good news of the kingdom, and healing every disease and every sickness. When He saw the crowds, He felt compassion for them, because they were weary and worn out,*

like sheep without a shepherd. Then He said to His disciples, "The harvest is abundant, but the workers are few. Therefore, pray to the Lord of the harvest to send out workers into His harvest" (MATTHEW 9:35–38).

The context of Jesus' instruction is important. Note the description of Jesus' work just prior to issuing this prayer challenge. Jesus was vigorously engaged in ministry. He was traveling through "all the towns and villages" while "teaching . . . preaching . . . and healing." The huge crowds with overwhelming needs moved Jesus with compassion—literally, "heart-rumbling." Jesus saw the people around Him as "weary and worn out, like sheep without a shepherd." From this brief summary, and our broader knowledge of Jesus' ministry, we know Jesus cared deeply and sacrificed much to reach people.

In light of how hard He was working, it seems Jesus would have issued a different directive than "pray." He might have said to His disciples, "You guys get busy. There's more to do than can be done by one man—even Me. At least get these crowds organized so I can work my way through them faster—getting to the most needy cases first. Come on, guys, look how hard I'm working. You've got to work harder. Let's get moving." But working harder, or even smarter, wasn't Jesus' agenda for the original disciples—or for you. Jesus knew the solution was getting more people—even more than the Twelve—to join Him in His work. Jesus knew His kingdom plan couldn't be accomplished by a few overworked disciples, but by many followers sharing the load. Jesus said to pray for more workers in the harvest.

Start by praying you will join the harvest in a fresh way. That's why you are reading this book—to more effectively live God's passion for reaching people with the gospel. So, in a sense, this prayer is already being answered—partially, perhaps in embryonic form, but slowly growing in your life. Pray you will be thoroughly devoted to God's mission and willing to make the lifestyle adjustments necessary to share your faith more intentionally. Pray you will join the harvest, not sit idly by hoping others will do it for you.

When you join the harvest, you will pray more earnestly for other Christians to help you. During Jesus' ministry, harvesting was a hands-on challenge. From grapes to grain, the work was done largely by manual labor. There were no tractors, combines, or trucks for hauling. Livestock were used but they also required care and feeding—again by hand. Harvesters in Jesus' time went into the fields, stayed from sunup to sundown, labored with crude tools, and suffered physically for it.

Imagine the difference between a first-century landowner (sitting in the shade, a cool breeze wafting by) and a field worker (bent at the waist, salty sweat burning his eyes). Who feels greater urgency to get the harvest concluded? My guess is the field worker. He wants to finish the job and rest from his labors. The landowner just wants to enjoy the results, and may drive the workers even harder as days go by. Both want the job finished, but one really feels the physical strain. Who do you think wants more help so the job will be done quicker? Again, the field worker. He longs for more harvesters—to shorten his days and complete the job before possible disaster strikes (weather, insects, etc.). While the landowner may fear loss of income from a diminished harvest, the field worker dreads the physical strain of backbreaking labor.

You will pray more passionately when you are involved in the harvest. Consider this scenario: A volunteer from a crisis pregnancy center makes a presentation in your church—reporting on the dire situations many young women face and the need to save babies from abortion. She asks for prayer for the center—for more workers and funding to expand the ministry. You bow your head while a pastor prays, agreeing with him for God to meet the needs. You even write a check and hand it to the volunteer on your way to your car. Once you leave the church, you probably won't think too much more about what you heard.

But suppose you were the volunteer making the presentation. When you wake up on Monday morning and kneel for prayer, do you think you will have any problem remembering to ask God for more volunteers (workers for the harvest) to join your work? Probably not. When you are in the field—feeling the heat, battling the challenges, racing against time—you will pray. You will pray naturally, spontaneously, passionately—without much prompting to keep you motivated. Harvesters pray harder than people sitting in the shade. When you actively engage lost people— whether among your circle of family and friends or in a people group you target—you will pray for them. You will also pray for more workers to join you in the important work of sharing the gospel in your community.

Have you ever considered what it will look like when your prayer for more harvesters is answered? For many years, my expectation about the answer to praying for "more workers" was off-base. My assumption was "more workers" meant more church members would join church-sponsored outreach efforts. Much energy was expended preaching, teaching, and challenging church members to support evangelism programs, ministry projects, and other attempts to reach people with the gospel. Certainly, this is one way a prayer for more workers may be answered. But there is another more profound source for additional workers in the harvest, and where those workers should be deployed. That source is the harvest itself.

FUTURE HARVESTERS AMONG THE HARVEST

When you share the gospel, the result will be people coming to faith in Jesus. As you disciple these new believers, part of your responsibility is helping them become colaborers in the harvest. One of the most misguided, even damaging approaches to discipleship, is telling a new Christians they "have a lot to learn" before they can "start sharing their faith." This is counterproductive on several levels. First, new believers have a passion that overcomes their lack of polish. Turn them loose and watch God minimize their innocent, inexperienced mistakes. Three weeks after his conversion, Kerry texted me, "When can I start telling people I'm a Christian?" I replied, "Today would be fine." Within minutes a mutual friend texted me about hearing the gospel from Kerry. He hasn't stopped sharing since. Kerry's authentic joy makes up for any lack of insight he may have about sharing the gospel.

A second reason to encourage new believers to share the gospel is they know a lot of lost people (most of their friends) and are often well known by them. The life change evident in a recent convert is a powerful testimony and a natural entrée into sharing the gospel. Their friends' curiosity about the changes they are observing leads naturally to talking about following Jesus.

Finally, new believers know and understand the community they have come from—its needs and problems—as well as its language and customs. In short, new believers naturally know how to interface with the people in their harvest field.

My friend Don works with Set Free Church in a major city in the western United States. The Set Free movement started among bikers—a rough and tough crowd. Don joined the work as an outsider, a Bible teacher invited by Set Free leadership to help stabilize their leadership structure. While he has been accepted by the group, his role is largely restricted to developing leaders. The most effective witnesses among the biker community are converted Set Free guys—not outsiders like Don. They have come to Christ from the biker culture—often formerly addicted to drugs, alcohol, or sex—as well as sometimes involved in criminal activity. They are tatted up, often with scars reminding them of past battles. These are the guys you don't want to meet on a dark night or have your daughter date. But now they wear T-shirts with sayings like, "To Hell with the Devil" and "Jesus Is Tougher than Hell" (they gave me one of those!). When it comes to reaching the biker community, Set Free guys are the best harvesters available. When Set Free Church prays for more harvesters, they don't pray for white, middle-class, suburban guys to start going to biker bars. Set Free believers pray for more converts from their community (out of the harvest) to go back to their community (into the harvest) with the gospel.

Whether its hockey moms, ballet dancers, race car drivers, or fraternity brothers, the best future harvesters are currently in the harvest. International missionaries know this and depend on implementing these principles. Their goal, when introducing the gospel in a new culture or community, is reaching a few nationals and then encouraging them to acculturate the gospel in their village, tribe, community, or caste. Once the gospel penetrates a community, the most rapid expansion usually occurs when outside influences are minimized and the harvested become the harvesters. Your first prayer related to personal evangelism is praying you will join the harvest. Then pray for more harvesters—but be sure you are praying while working in the field, not relaxing on the porch.

PRAY FOR MORE OPPORTUNITIES TO SHARE THE GOSPEL

A door is a frequent biblical image used to communicate spiritual truth. For example, Jesus said, "Listen! I stand at the door and knock.

PRAY FOR SPIRITUAL ALERTNESS TO RECOGNIZE THOSE OPPORTUNITIES WHEN THEY COME.

If anyone hears My voice and opens the door, I will come in to him and have dinner with him, and he with Me" (Revelation 3:20).

When Paul wrote to his friends in Colossae, he asked them to pray for him to have more opportunities to share the gospel. He used the door motif when he wrote, "At the same time, pray also for us that God may open a door to us for the message, to speak the mystery of the Messiah" (Colossians 4:3). There are two aspects to this prayer request. First, Paul asked his friends to pray he would have more witnessing opportunities. Second, he asked for prayer to keep his witness focused on Jesus.

The image of a door symbolizing opportunity or responsibility is common to many cultures. When a door is opened for an arriving guest, it initiates new opportunities to enjoy friends. When a door is opened for a departing family member, he or she leaves for new responsibilities. When Paul asked the Colossians to pray "that God may open a door to us for the message," he was asking them to pray for two things—first, for additional witnessing opportunities; second, for spiritual alertness to those opportunities. In other words, continuing the door metaphor, Paul asked for prayer to recognize when opportunity to share the gospel was knocking.

Based on this biblical prayer request, it's appropriate to ask God to create witnessing opportunities for you. You should also pray for spiritual alertness to recognize those opportunities when they come. Becoming dull about these matters can happen to anyone.

I lead a Bible study for baseball players. I am also praying for other players, who may not yet be believers, to become Christians. I am praying for opportunities to talk with them about Jesus. One day, during Bible study, one of the players I had been praying for knocked on the door (literally) to our meeting room. I was slow getting to the door, so he had walked to the end of the hall before I answered it. I saw him disappear around the corner. I thought, *I wonder who knocked on the door?* and then went back to the group. Just as I sat down, the player knocked on the door again.

When I opened it, he asked, "Is this Bible study?"

"Yes," I replied, not moving from the doorway.

After a few awkward seconds, he said, "Well, can I come in?" At that moment, I realized two things—God was answering my prayer, and I was a spiritual dullard. I had been praying for a "door to open" into this guy's life, and when he literally knocked on a door and asked to study the Bible with me—all I could do was wonder why he was standing there. After Bible study he stayed after for further conversation in which I (finally alert to his interest) shared the gospel with him.

You should pray for God to open doors—to create witnessing opportunities for you. But also pray for spiritual alertness to know when the door has opened. Sometimes, we become so preoccupied we can't hear the tapping—or pounding—of a person who is ready to hear the gospel.

What do these open doors look like? How can you know someone might be open to hearing about Jesus? The following phrases help me: *people die, health fails, relationships struggle,* and *things break.* When any of these unfortunate events happen (and they happen to everyone at one time or another), people are often open to hearing the gospel. These life events become doors of opportunity for talking about Jesus. Being attuned to these four "doors" has been the most helpful new concept about personal evangelism I have learned in the past decade. For many years, I stewed over how to introduce Jesus into ongoing relationships. My past attempts were often awkward, even sometimes seeming manipulative. Now, that's not the case. By simply paying attention as life happens to people, and stepping in with the gospel when one of these four circumstances occurs, sharing Jesus has become a natural part of many conversations.

Keeping the focus on Jesus is the second part of Paul's prayer request. He asked his friends to pray he would "speak the mystery of the Messiah." In other words, keep the focus on Jesus. You should pray you will keep Jesus—His person and work—foremost in your witness to others. Too often, our encounters with lost people detour from Jesus down side roads and back alleys. Getting sidetracked by focusing on a person's sinful behavior, external issues not germane to the gospel, or even positive subjects like church programs can short-circuit your witness. Keep the focus on Jesus. In the next chapter, we will discover why this is so difficult and how to solve the problem. For now, focus on praying for spiritual self-discipline to avoid chasing rabbits like secular politics, denominational differences, or negative aspects of other religious groups. Pray you will keep Jesus at the forefront of your witness. When opportunity knocks, open the door and invite the person to meet Jesus—not every other person, problem, or perspective in the room.

PRAY FOR BOLD INSIGHT FOR SHARING THE GOSPEL

Sharing the gospel today is challenging for many reasons. Supernatural opposition seems stronger than ever. People are coming from increasingly more diverse and muddled religious backgrounds. Many people are very spiritual, having concocted a brew of beliefs by dipping from multiple religious pots. Paul lived in a world like ours, so he wrote the Ephesians:

> *Pray also for me, that the message may be given to me when I open my mouth to make known with boldness the mystery of the gospel. . . . Pray that I might be bold enough in Him to speak as I should* (EPHESIANS 6:19–20).

There are two concerns expressed in this prayer request. First, Paul asked for prayer so that he would know what to say when he spoke ("the message may be given to me when I open my mouth"). Second, he asked twice for prayer that he would speak boldly ("make known with boldness" and "be bold enough").

Pray for wisdom to share the gospel in today's world. In past years, many witness training events devoted considerable time to helping Christians learn answers to questions or objections non-Christians might raise. While that training approach still has merit, religious pluralism today makes it difficult to learn responses to the variety of potential issues which might emerge in a witnessing conversation. Rather than trying to learn "all the answers," your time is better spent mastering the gospel and how to apply it effectively to the needs of the person you are talking with. Then, in the moment, trust God to help you to speak wisely during dialogue about Jesus.

Bella had an eating disorder. When we met, it was hard to look past her emaciated condition and discover her deepest need. Frankly, her situation was way beyond my expertise and comfort level. As we talked about her struggles, it seemed wise to focus on God's love and acceptance as the key message for her. When I explained God's unconditional love, she was so moved she started crying—deep, gut-wrenching sobs coming from an emotional depth I wasn't expecting

SHE STARTED CRYING—
DEEP, GUT-WRENCHING SOBS.

to plumb. After a few minutes, she prayed to commit her life to Jesus. My strong impression, throughout our conversation, was the importance of focusing on God's love as the key ingredient she needed to understand about the gospel.

Another day, a friend told me about his ongoing adulterous relationship. Rather than focus on God's love, it seemed wiser to confront him, warning him of God's judgment (the pain he would experience from the consequences of his actions) and ultimate separation from God (for eternity, if he refused to repent). I don't like confrontation—who really does?—but it had to be done. He needed a firm reminder of God's standards and his need to repent and seek forgiveness. Both with Bella and my adulterous friend, the conversation took a direction I didn't and couldn't anticipate. Praying for wisdom—in the moment, on the spot—is essential for tailoring your message to each person's unique situation.

You must also pray for boldness to share the gospel, particularly to introduce Jesus into the conversation. Have you noticed how controversial it is to talk about Jesus? On television, for example, when prayer is depicted—even by Christians—it's usually offered to God without adding "in Jesus' name." A few years ago, I was asked to pray at a community event. The only admonition was to avoid controversy—translation: pray a generic, inoffensive prayer without mentioning Jesus. It requires boldness to overcome cultural pressure and talk about Jesus. The need for boldness isn't new to our culture. In the early days of the church, they prayed, "Lord, consider their threats, and grant that Your slaves may speak Your message with complete boldness" (Acts 4:29). Not much has changed in 2,000 years. Pray for God to give you boldness to speak the name of Jesus, and also to pray in His name no matter how controversial that may be to some people.

PRAY FOR THE GOSPEL TO SPREAD RAPIDLY

Are you frustrated more people aren't being saved through your church or as a result of your witness? Most of us are! The slow pace of gospel growth in many settings makes it seem this is a normal, acceptable pattern. It's not. Paul wrapped up his correspondence with the Thessalonians by writing, "Finally, pray for us, brothers, that the Lord's message may spread rapidly and be honored"

(2 Thessalonians 3:1). His request was for rapid, honorable expansion of the gospel. We can pray the same prayer for our generation.

False gospels—like the prosperity gospel—seem to be spreading more rapidly than the true gospel. This isn't honorable gospel expansion. When the true gospel spreads rapidly, Jesus is exalted, true discipleship demanded, and selfless service results. More rapid expansion of the true gospel may seem like a formidable, even impossible, goal. But praying for it is our privilege and responsibility. We can't settle for less.

The growth of the gospel across Africa (where people are coming to Jesus in waves) can be traced to the focused praying of thousands of Christians—like my mother-in-law who has maintained a lifelong passion for praying the gospel across Africa. The same can be said for Korea, a nation with a burgeoning Christian population fueled by their practice of early morning prayer meetings. Gospel expansion is tied to fervent praying. The results come slowly at first but crescendo later as the cumulative effect of prayers by many are answered in subsequent generations.

Do you have an unsaved family member who seems antagonistic to the gospel? Pray! Do you want the trickle of converts coming into your church to turn into a flood? Pray! Do you long for sweeping revival across our nation? Pray! While these things seem impossible, remember, "You do not have because you do not ask" (James 4:2) and, "With God all things are possible" (Matthew 19:26). Rapid expansion of the gospel may seem impossible, but it's not. Perhaps God is waiting on your prayers to initiate a fresh harvest in your family, church, community, or country. Hit your knees and ask for what seems impossible.

PRAY FOR PEOPLE TO BE SAVED

Praying for people groups (communities, tribes, or nations) and praying for individuals to be saved is biblical. Simply and directly asking for the conversion of a person or group follows Paul's example. He wrote one of his prayers when he exclaimed, "Brothers, my heart's desire and prayer to God concerning them (Israel) is for their salvation!" (Romans 10:1). While Paul sensed God's call primarily to evangelize Gentiles (see chap. 1), he still wanted his own people—

Hebrews—to follow Jesus. So, he prayed for Israel to come to Jesus. This has many layers of application.

First, pray for nations, tribes, or people groups to be saved. One of the most helpful global mission strategies, which has intensified in the past two decades, is praying for people groups to respond to the gospel. When a class, small group, or church takes on a project like this, their spiritual preparation precedes and accompanies missionaries who engage those cultures.

Second, pray for communities or subgroups within communities to be saved. You can pray for the students in your classroom, the people who work in your office, or the fellows in the jail you visit. Any defined subset of people can be an object of your intercession.

Third, pray for individuals, by name, to be saved. Make a list of friends and family members and pray for them to be saved. Asking God for their conversion, by name, is like hand-to-hand spiritual warfare. By praying for people one-by-one, you confront spiritual bondage and oppose forces that confuse them and limit their responsiveness to God. Paul described it this way:

> *For although we are walking in the flesh, we do not wage war in a fleshly way, since the weapons of our warfare are not fleshly, but are powerful through God for the demolition of strongholds. We demolish arguments and every high-minded thing that is raised up against the knowledge of God, taking every thought captive to the obedience of Christ* (2 CORINTHIANS 10:3–5).

One way to increase your praying for individuals is to make a list of unsaved people and pray for them regularly. My current prayer list has several men, mostly friends met through baseball, who I am praying will be saved. My prayers for them, while contributing to their spiritual openness, also remind me to look for opportunities to share the gospel with them. Praying for the lost—whether a people group or as individuals—sensitizes you to their needs, increases your burden for their conversion, and motivates you to tell them about Jesus. It's difficult to remain callous toward people you are consistently praying will be saved.

One man was behaving badly, his lostness expressing itself in immoral choices jeopardizing his marriage and family. He was resistant to God and unresponsive to efforts to talk with him about his choices and their results. Then a few of us started praying—hard. We prayed for other believers among his acquaintances to speak the gospel to him, for wisdom to know how to talk with him about Jesus, for boldness to confront him about his destructive behavior, and for him to be saved. After a few months, he called a Christian friend, talked to him for almost three hours, and then received Jesus as his Lord and Savior.

The change was immediate and dramatic. He became a Bible study junkie, asked dozens of questions about how to align his life with what he was learning from Scripture, made a herculean effort to restore his marriage, and stopped destructive lifestyle habits. *Transformation* is too bland a word to describe what happened. *Miracle* is a better choice! When a few of us committed to pray, God intervened and changed a life. Your prayers aligned with God's will (based on the models and instructions in this chapter) access God's power to change people.

A SIMPLE LIST, SOME SIMPLE STEPS

The five biblical passages mentioned in this chapter produce a short list of strategic and specific prayers to increase your evangelistic effectiveness. Since these prayer requests emerge directly from Scripture, you can be sure they are according to God's will. Pray them with confidence and expect God to answer.

- Pray for yourself to be more involved sharing your faith.
- Pray for other believers to join you working in the harvest.
- Pray for more opportunities to witness.
- Pray for spiritual discipline to keep your witness focused on Jesus.
- Pray for wisdom to witness effectively—no matter the situation you may face.
- Pray for boldness to talk about Jesus.
- Pray for the gospel to spread rapidly.
- Pray for people—specific groups and individuals—to be saved.

How can you shape your praying toward these requests? Two simple steps will help. First, write these prayer requests on a card, in your prayer journal, or on the back of your prayer list. When you pray, personalize these requests to your situation and to individuals. Don't worry about using exact words. These requests aren't a mantra or a magic formula. They are, however, important guides to shape your praying toward God's will. There's also nothing wrong with using a prayer list and written prayers—even praying with your eyes open and reading your prayer if necessary. Suppose you are praying for a friend named Jack to be saved. Your prayer might sound something like this:

> *Heavenly Father, help me witness to Jack and motivate other believers who know him to also tell him about Jesus. Give me an opportunity to witness to Jack, and help me focus on Jesus when we talk. I'm afraid to witness sometimes, please make me bolder. Finally, Father, please save Jack, and save him as soon as possible.*

This sample prayer is saturated with God's will because it's based on biblical instructions, examples, and models. Pray this way with confidence.

A second suggestion to shape your praying is memorizing the Scripture passages upon which the five prayers outlined in this chapter are based (Matthew 9:35–38; Colossians 4:3; Ephesians 6:19–20; 2 Thessalonians 3:1; and Romans 10:1). You can also memorize 1 John 5:14–15 for further encouragement.

God answers prayers offered according to His will. By memorizing these passages, you will internalize truth about prayer. It will shape your thinking and the way you pray. As an added bonus, you will have this "prayer guide" with you all the time. Even when you aren't in your prayer place with your prayer list, you will find yourself praying according to these memorized models. But however you pray—pray much and pray often!

A marine and his friend were burdened for the spiritual condition of the men in their barracks. When they attempted to share the gospel, they were rebuffed, ridiculed, or ended up in arguments. They changed their strategy from trying to share the gospel to just trying to get some guys to at least go to church with them. They spent four months extending invitations, putting up flyers, and helping with barracks duties to create free time for the men to possibly attend church—to no avail. They gave up, took down the flyers, and "decided just to pray for them." Within a month, they needed two cars to get everyone to church who wanted to go. Prayer worked when every other effort failed.

Pray for the advance of the gospel. Pray strategically and specifically, using the insights in this chapter as a guide. Prayer is the essential foundation for accelerating the fulfillment of the Great Commission. But after laying this foundation, what do you place on it? The building material for expanding God's kingdom is the gospel. The message you share is vital to the process of making disciples of irreligious people. We have already seen, in one of the prayer requests in this chapter, a reference to speaking about Jesus. He is the central figure in your witness. He is the focal point of the gospel. Let's turn our attention to honing our message, an essential ingredient for effectively talking with people about Jesus.

CHAPTER 3

STAYING
ON MESSAGE

P UBLIC FIGURES STAY ON MESSAGE when giving
interviews or making speeches. Staying on message means,
no matter the venue or question, information is communicated with minimal distraction or dilution. Staying on message
also means relating any question back to the core message. Media
consultants earn large salaries making sure their clients master
these important skills. Too often, however, in the public arena these
efforts manipulate information and situations to further an agenda.
Witnessing Christians, like public figures, must stay on message. But
our determination to stay on message must be devoid of duplicity or
selfishness. Our message mandates a pure-hearted effort.

What is our message? *The gospel!* This part of personal
evangelism *is* scripted. We aren't commissioned to spread
spiritual platitudes. We don't make up our message. The good news
about Jesus is our message. We aren't satisfied until we have
communicated the gospel effectively to people we are trying to reach.
It requires discipline to stay on message about the gospel. Doing
less compromises Christianity's core message, as well as dilutes and

diminishes the eternal nature of our message. When you do kind things for people—even motivated by your devotion to Jesus, but without communicating the gospel—your efforts aren't much different than those of a secular social worker. Your motive may be pure, your methods sound, and people may be helped in concrete ways. But if the gospel isn't communicated, your work is temporal—lacking an eternal dimension as well as the capacity to change lives now. The gospel is our central message. Communicating it is our responsibility and privilege.

Many messages compete with and substitute for the gospel—including other good information delivered by well-meaning believers. For example, some Christians focus on the effects of the gospel—peace of mind, power to make better choices, or improved relationships as their core message. They say things like, "Jesus will help you have a better life. Just ask Him." Another common mistake is substituting invitations to spiritual activities like "Come to church" or "Join my Bible study" for presenting the gospel. Inviting a friend to church or a Bible study group can be a positive step—but it isn't the same as sharing the gospel. Communicating a jargon-size or truncated gospel is another common mistake. Phrases like *God loves you* or *Give your heart to Jesus* are true, but assuming unbelievers understand these truth-snippets and can somehow piece together the rest of the story isn't wise. Given the general lack of biblical literacy today, this outcome is highly unlikely.

Staying on message means you understand the gospel, can communicate it clearly, do so in appropriate ways, and in a timely fashion. It also means you don't equate general spiritual comments with the gospel message of salvation. To help you stay on message, let's answer the fundamental question about your core message. By doing so, we will discover the scripted part of an unscripted approach to personal evangelism.

WHAT IS THE GOSPEL?

The gospel, defined by its root word, is "good news." It's the good news about salvation in Jesus Christ. Many creeds and confessions, adopted by various Christian churches, councils, or denominations over the centuries have summarized the gospel. One recent example adopted by Southern Baptists is *The Baptist Faith and Message 2000*,

IT *IS* IMPORTANT TO COMMUNICATE KEY ASPECTS OF THIS SUMMARY WHEN YOU PRESENT THE GOSPEL.

a statement that includes a comprehensive and balanced summary of the gospel. Read through it carefully and then let's consider how to use this information in everyday conversations.

Salvation involves the redemption of the whole man, and is offered freely to all who accept Jesus Christ as Lord and Savior, who by His own blood obtained eternal redemption for the believer. In its broadest sense salvation includes regeneration, justification, sanctification, and glorification. There is no salvation apart from personal faith in Jesus Christ as Lord.

A. Regeneration, or the new birth, is a work of God's grace whereby believers become new creatures in Christ Jesus. It is a change of heart wrought by the Holy Spirit through conviction of sin, to which the sinner responds in repentance toward God and faith in the Lord Jesus Christ. Repentance and faith are inseparable experiences of grace. Repentance is a genuine turning from sin toward God. Faith is the acceptance of Jesus Christ and commitment of the entire personality to Him as Lord and Savior.

B. Justification is God's gracious and full acquittal upon principles of His righteousness of all sinners who repent and believe in Christ. Justification brings the believer unto a relationship of peace and favor with God.

C. Santification is the experience, beginning in regeneration, by which the believer is set apart to God's purposes, and is enabled to progress toward moral and spiritual maturity through the presence and power of the Holy Spirit dwelling in him. Growth in grace should continue throughout the regenerate person's life.

D. Glorification is the culmination of salvation and is the final blessed and abiding state of the redeemed.

That's a mouthful! Fortunately, sharing the gospel doesn't mean memorizing these paragraphs and repeating them to every unbeliever you meet. This is a comprehensive statement about salvation, summarizing the gospel's effects from new birth to eternal life. It uses technical language—both biblical and theological—that might even hinder the gospel being understood by an unbeliever unfamiliar with this terminology. While it isn't essential to recite these paragraphs verbatim, it *is* important to communicate key aspects of this summary when you present the gospel. It's also equally important, even though the entire statement is seldom used in conversation, that no part of it be contradicted or minimized by what is presented.

Communicating the gospel in everyday language (while preserving the robust theological insights) might sound like this:

✝

God loves you and wants you to have the best life possible. Something called sin stands in your way. Being a sinner doesn't mean you always make the worst choices possible. It simply means, no matter how hard you try, you can't come up to God's standards. No matter how hard you try, you are still living for yourself, which never pleases God. You need forgiveness and that's only possible if someone pays the penalty for your sin.

The good news is Jesus died on the Cross in your place to do just that! He died, but then three days later came back alive from the dead. By doing this, He showed He is more powerful than sin and its result—death. Jesus is the only person in history who ever died and was raised back from the dead—never to die again.

Now, you must decide about Jesus. If you turn away from your sin and from living for yourself, He will forgive you and give you a brand-new life. Your decision is simple. You must trust Jesus as your Savior from sin and submit yourself to Him as your new Lord. Once you make this decision, you will be changed immediately on the inside. Then, over time, as you learn to follow Jesus by obeying His instructions in the Bible, your entire life will change.

The best part of all—someday you will be with Jesus and God and every other person who has ever followed Jesus in heaven, forever!

✝

This short summary, like the preceding theological statement, isn't meant to be memorized and delivered like a speech. This is just an example of how you might translate the gospel into plain language, devoid of religious terminology and jargon, for a secular hearer. Depending on the background of the other person in the dialogue, you should adjust your presentation so they can understand it fully. You are a translator, communicating profound truth in understandable terms. The goal is clear communication without compromising the true meaning of the gospel.

One way to establish a gospel-baseline for witnessing is memorizing a short gospel presentation. Yes, memorize! There's great value in witness training programs that include memorizing Scripture verses, summary statements explaining key aspects of the gospel, and simple illustrations to clarify the concepts. Learning a gospel-script, if you want to think of it that way, is like memorizing multiplication tables. When you memorize multiplication facts, they become ingrained in how you think about numbers. Without much effort, you can recall multiplication facts and apply them in a variety of life situations. When you memorize a gospel presentation, you can do the same thing. You won't repeat it verbatim in every conversation, but you can draw on what you know and make appropriate use of it in any conversational situation.

On stage, an actor works from a script. But the best acting occurs when the script is internalized and becomes part of the character. The words come alive, not delivered like a recited assignment, but as realistically as if there had never been a script. Personal evangelism can draw from a scripted understanding of the gospel, while personalizing it appropriately in gospel-connected, unscripted conversations.

Sometimes, even the full script works just fine. Gary memorized a lengthy gospel presentation as part of a witness training program at our church. He spent weeks learning it perfectly—every verse, concept, and illustration. We visited in the home of two sisters who had attended our church. I asked if Gary could share with them what he had been learning in a class at church. They agreed. Gary hit the mental play button and delivered the entire memorized presentation—for 20 minutes—word for word. The longer he talked, the more I cringed. I was sure the two women would be put off by such a canned approach. When Gary finished, I asked, "What questions do you have?" One of the women said, "No questions. That was the clearest thing I have ever heard!" A few minutes later she prayed with us to receive Jesus as her Savior and Lord (and was later baptized at our church). While I don't recommend it as a preferred approach, even delivering a gospel monologue can be effective in communicating the gospel.

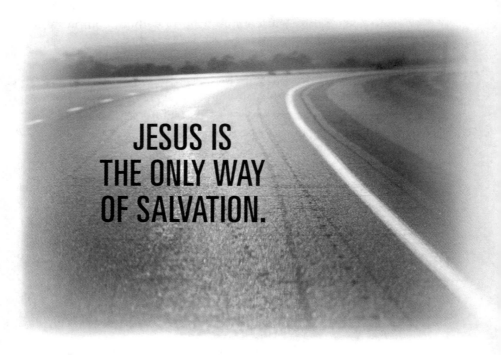

JESUS IS
THE ONLY WAY
OF SALVATION.

GENERATIONAL CHALLENGES TODAY

Isolating specific aspects of the gospel for special consideration is a subjective decision fraught with risk. But in every generation, certain aspects must be emphasized to adequately communicate the gospel in light of present challenges. In most cultures today, the following four issues are paramount for communicating the gospel and require special emphasis in witnessing encounters.

Jesus is the only way of salvation. The most controversial aspect of the gospel is Jesus is the only way of salvation. The historical Jesus, as revealed and described in the New Testament, is the central person of the gospel. Jesus is more than a teacher, prophet, moral example, or idealized man. He is the Son of God—crucified, resurrected, ascended—and salvation is not possible apart from Jesus.

Salvation is received, not achieved. Salvation is offered to all who repent from sin and place faith in Jesus. The qualifiers for receiving salvation are repentance and faith. When, by the grace of God, any person repents of sin and places faith in Jesus, salvation results. No human effort, no matter how religiously devoted or spiritually motivated, contributes to salvation. Good works, no matter how well-intended, don't contribute to salvation.

Salvation is available to everyone. Salvation is available to any person—from any culture, language, tribe, or nation. Anyone and everyone who repents from sin and believes in Jesus will be saved. No one knows who will be saved; rather, our responsibility is to tell everyone about the opportunity for salvation. The gospel is for everyone.

Salvation affects the entire person. The gospel produces initial change (regeneration/ justification), continual change (sanctification), and ultimate change (glorification). When you present the gospel, you must not minimize the lifestyle changes the gospel demands and produces. Anything less is a distorted gospel with a detrimental effect on the person who receives it.

Christians share the gospel. That's our message. Doing so is a significant challenge today—for several reasons—but this isn't a new problem. From the earliest days of the Christian movement, the gospel's purity has been threatened. How quickly did this problem arise? Believe it or not, while the first generation of Christians were still alive!

STRUGGLES FROM THE START

Galatians was likely the first letter Paul sent to a church or group of churches. Assuming it was written in the early AD 50s, that's only about 25 years after the Resurrection. This means some believers who were part of Jesus' earthly ministry were still alive. Yet, those early Christians—who may have known Jesus personally—struggled to hold to the true gospel. Paul summarized the gospel this way for the Galatians:

> *Grace to you and peace from God the Father and our Lord Jesus Christ, who gave Himself for our sins to rescue us from this present evil age, according to the will of our God and Father, to whom be the glory forever and ever. Amen* (GALATIANS 1:3–5).

This is a robust, soaring exaltation of the gospel—followed by a hearty *amen* (meaning, "so let it be"). But while the amen is still ringing in the air, notice the next incredible statement: "I am amazed that you are so quickly turning away from Him who called you by the grace of Christ, and are turning to a different gospel" (Galatians 1:6).

A different gospel? Already? Just one generation after Jesus? Amazingly, yes. This distortion of the gospel was related to circumcision as an act of covenant keeping with God (Galatians 5:7–12; Acts 15) and its relationship to salvation. The story of the church's struggle with this issue is fascinating, but far beyond the scope of this book. Suffice it to say, the crisis was resolved effectively—preserving both the theological integrity and practical fellowship of the church.

Our purpose in considering this early example of confusion about the gospel isn't to analyze the specific situation, but to recognize the long and persistent struggle to maintain the gospel's purity. The battle has raged since soon after the Resurrection, continues to our generation, and will persist until Jesus returns. Maintaining allegiance to the gospel has two dimensions—theological and personal. The first is usually thought of as more challenging. The second, not as difficult. For most Christians, the opposite is true. We courageously establish doctrinal convictions, but struggle with the relational tension created by sharing them.

SOMETIMES, THE CHALLENGES ARE THEOLOGICAL

Theological challenges to the gospel arise both inside and outside the church. As previously mentioned, the problem in the first century was the relationship of circumcision to the gospel. This may seem like an arcane problem, but to first-generation believers emerging from centuries of Jewish practice, it was a major concern. Christians face different challenges today. External pressures include post-modernism, relativism, and religious pluralism. Inside the church, we struggle with liberal theology and compromise rooted in false notions of unity. Overarching all this is a growing aversion to authority and rejection of absolute truth. As a Christian, you are floating on a sea of theological and philosophical perspectives undermining the gospel. You must be on the lookout for currents drifting you away from the gospel mainstream.

Paul issued warnings about three sources of theological error concerning the gospel in his day. They are still important in ours. You probably believe the gospel (or you wouldn't be reading a book about sharing it more effectively). Convincing you about the gospel probably isn't necessary. Instead, let's focus on the sources of error that might cause you to drift from gospel orthodoxy (the same sources unbelievers often listen to as authentic). Confronting these sources of false information is sometimes part of conversing about the gospel.

The first source of potential error is anonymous experts. Paul wrote, "There are some who are troubling you and want to change the gospel of Christ" (Galatians 1:7). "Some who are troubling you"—nameless, faceless, anonymous know-it-alls who expound religious opinion. They litter the blogosphere and the coffee shop with comments like, "Everyone knows all religions lead to God; it doesn't matter what you believe, as long as you are sincere; God is love and all of us are His children; God helps those who help themselves; and my Jesus would never send anyone to hell." These statements are pop culture contradictions of the gospel. They have no sound theological or philosophical foundation, yet serve as presumptive conclusions for many. When someone says something like this to me, my response is to ask, "What's your basis for that belief?" The answer, in one form or another, is almost always the same—"It just feels right to me." If there is an external source, it's usually, "I heard it on the radio"; "read it on the Internet"; "heard a minister say one time"; or some other anonymous reference. The problem with this drivel is, repeated often enough, it takes on an air of credibility. Be on guard lest anonymous experts dilute your convictions about the gospel.

A second source of confusion about the gospel is more difficult to admit. Paul warned, "But even if we . . . should preach to you a gospel other than what we have preached to you" (Galatians 1:8). By including himself—referencing "we"—Paul meant Christian leaders can be the problem. Some so-called Christian leaders are sources of error about the gospel. It's easy in our media-driven culture to confuse popularity with accuracy, marketing expertise with theological soundness. As a Christian, you should learn from leaders who are pioneering new ways to communicate the gospel but not those adjusting the message to make it more palatable. This is a delicate, but significant distinction. Christian leaders who are innovating new methods to spread an accurate gospel should be applauded. We need fresh thinking to meet today's spiritual challenges to the gospel. But be on guard! When any leader, no matter how prominent, preaches or teaches a "new" gospel, confront and reject the error. Every Christian must understand the gospel well enough to recognize and reject false versions of it—no matter how popular the source.

Finally, the third source of confusion about the gospel might seem an unlikely problem today. Paul warned not even to believe "an angel from heaven" who preached a false gospel (Galatians 1:8). You may be thinking, "No problem. No angels are preaching in my community."

While that's true, look deeper into the origins of religious movements before you determine there's no threat to the gospel from this source. Almost every major world religion or Christian cult traces its origin to some form of supernatural revelation (delivered by angelic or heavenly messenger). Consider two prominent examples. Islam originated when Muhammad received a heavenly vision. The Church of Jesus Christ of Latter-day Saints (the Mormons) traces its roots to new revelation (The Book of Mormon) resulting from angelic direction. The greatest threats to the gospel today, worldwide, in almost every case originated with some form of "angelic" revelation.

Despite the confusion about and challenges to the gospel in today's world, you have believed and received the gospel. It's a settled conviction for you. You really want to share it. Your greatest limitation to doing so isn't doctrinal. It's something else, something more personal and frankly, much more difficult to overcome.

THE GREATER CHALLENGE IS RELATIONAL

While Paul warned the Galatians about succumbing to theological error, he ended his plea for purity about the gospel by describing a more pressing problem. He asked two probing questions, "For am I now trying to win the favor of people, or God? Or am I striving to please people?" (Galatians 1:10). The uncomfortable awkwardness that silences many Christians is the relational tension that results from sharing the gospel. We want people to like us—and the gospel often unsettles those affections.

Sharing the gospel can create tension in relationships for many reasons. First, when you share the gospel you move beyond superficial small talk to significant life issues. This can be threatening if not handled properly. The gospel connects with the core of a person's needs, choices, and private concerns. The gospel lays bare closely guarded secrets—passions and pains often buried beneath layers of carefully constructed coping mechanisms. Like Pandora's box, once it's opened, the contents spill out and the results aren't easily contained.

A friend had been sharing the gospel with Mary, who agreed to meet with me for more in-depth conversation. With just a few probing questions, several specific issues surfaced as the pressing concerns driving her to consider major life changes. But when I explained faith as "trusting God," her response was startling. Like a dentist finding a raw nerve, my question connected with her deepest pain. She erupted in a two-hour litany about the broken promises in her marriage. Her capacity to trust God—to trust anyone—had been shattered by her husband's destructive behavior. Our quiet conversation turned into spiritual triage—just trying to stop the bleeding long enough to describe how God could heal the wound. Mary exhausted her pain through the cathartic experience of telling me her story. A few weeks later she committed her life to Jesus and, thankfully, so did her husband. Their marriage, over time, was healed as a result.

But the point of this story isn't the happy ending; it's learning to manage the painful process of connecting the gospel to a person's deepest need. Prepare yourself for emotionally draining moments when you share the gospel. Unbelievers often have painful experiences in their past (or present) either prohibiting them from considering the gospel or driving them to it. Either way, it can be emotionally draining—for both parties in the conversation. When you share the gospel, relational tension may also include sharing another person's pain while keeping your emotions in check. This can be a difficult challenge.

A man brought his teenage daughter to see me. He was a prominent businessman and member of a church in another denomination. His daughter was pregnant and he was too embarrassed to go to their pastor. As he talked, his daughter sat in front of me, never looking up, tears dropping into her lap. The more her father talked about her sin, his disappointment, his embarrassment, and how he wanted me to confront her for what she had done, the lower she sank into her chair and the angrier I became. She needed a strong father to stand with her; instead she had a whining coward only concerned about his reputation in the community. Setting aside my anger, making a ministry action plan for this young woman, and sharing the gospel with them was difficult.

On another occasion, a woman approached me for help—bruises on her neck and face from a recent beating by her husband. Helping her was step one. Beating up her husband seemed like a good step two! Spousal abuse is despicable. Then, a few days later, her husband also came to me for help. He wasn't a Christian and needed to hear the gospel. Honestly, and this is painful to write, I held him in such low regard it was hard to tell him about Jesus. I wanted him judged, not forgiven. Setting aside anger, frustration, bitterness, resentment, and judgmental feelings is essential for sharing the gospel with sinners who disclose their ugliest behavior to us.

A second reason the gospel produces interpersonal tension is it confronts a person's sin. As the gospel's messenger, angry response to conviction of sin may be taken out on you. Even if you make a winsome, gentle gospel presentation, you may still find yourself in the line of fire. Bobby brought up the gospel, asking questions about following Jesus. When he learned he was a sinner and repentance was required, the tone of the conversation changed abruptly. Rather than becoming more open to the gospel, he became surly and defensive. He accused me of being judgmental and God of being hateful. His bluster only masked his vulnerability. The message about sin pained him, but he was unwilling to repent.

Jay also reacted negatively when confronted with his sin. When he learned the Bible says, "All have sinned," he replied, "I've got you right there. I'm better than most church people I know." He was right, in one sense. He was a very moral man. But when Jesus (not his churchgoing friends) was pointed out as the only standard of righteousness, the conversation came to a halt. He did not want to talk about how his life stacked up against Jesus'.

Both these men reacted negatively to any mention they were sinners—one with significant anger, the other with polite but firm debate. Neither of these conversations ended with a conversion. Both left me frustrated. Sometimes, no matter how gentle the witness, conviction about sin still produces resistance.

Being ridiculed for believing the gospel is a third form of relational tension felt by Christians. One of the first questions Tom asked when he learned I was a Christian was, "Do you really believe Jesus is the only way of salvation?" Before I could answer, he added, "And do you think people who don't follow Jesus go to hell when they die?" Yes and yes. While those were the answers he expected, for Tom they were the wrong answers. He sneered, "You seem like such a bright guy. How can you believe such nonsense?" before adding, "God loves people too much to allow only one way of salvation and would never send anyone to hell." My attempts to explain my reasons were dismissed out of hand. His opinion of my intelligence and credibility were diminished that day. Being belittled was painful.

When you share the gospel, some will ridicule you. You may be called a narrow-minded, Bible-thumping fundamentalist. You may be accused of being intolerant or judgmental. Your intelligence or compassion may be questioned. If you explain or defend your convictions, you may be accused of being argumentative or prejudiced. The verbal rebukes may intensify as anger erupts and poisons not only the conversation, but the relationship.

Being ridiculed about the gospel can lead to outright rejection of any further dialogue about it. A person may ask you not to speak about Jesus any more in their presence, stop inviting him to church, or otherwise end any spiritual conversations in her presence. One person told me, "I don't even want you praying for me."

Shortly after he became a Christian, Mark spent the weekend with a good friend. They had roomed together for three years in college, shared football season tickets to their alma mater, and Mark had been the best man in all three of his friend's weddings. When his friend commented Mark "seemed different," he shared the gospel with him. His friend replied, "Well, I guess I respect you for that, but you have to respect me for not believing that way." Since then, they have had limited contact—not because Mark wanted to end a friendship, but because the other person has cut off the relationship. The gospel can come between you and your closest friends.

Going beyond relational tension to rejection is painful. If you have a roommate who has told you not to talk to them about Jesus, a grandchild who argues with you when you present the gospel, an employee who threatens legal action if you witness in the workplace, a spouse who promises to leave if you continue to "jam Jesus down my throat," or a former friend who avoids you because of your faith, you know it hurts! These are people you care about and want to relate to positively. You love them and want them to have meaningful life now and eternal life later. Seeing someone you care about turn his or her back on the gospel, and on you, is painful. Rejection stings!

YOU ARE NOT THE PROBLEM

Relational tension occasionally results from insensitive or overbearing attempts to share the gospel. That's inexcusable. If you are witnessing that way, stop it! You are responsible to share the gospel winsomely, with as much love, tact, and deference to others as possible. Most Christians who witness do so with gentleness and love. The old saying about "beating someone over the head with the Bible" is a caricature, an anomaly seldom seen among caring Christians. But even when you present the gospel effectively and compassionately, relational tension may still occur. Why does this happen?

The first reason for unsettling responses to the gospel is conviction brought by the Holy Spirit during your witness. The Holy Spirit "will convict the world about sin, righteousness, and the judgment: about sin, because they do not believe in Me" (John 16:8–9). This conviction can come through many means—but one is important for this study. As a Christian indwelled by the Spirit (and filled with the Spirit while witnessing), you are an agent through whom the Spirit convicts others. That's why unbelievers are sometimes uncomfortable just being in your presence, even if there isn't a gospel presentation. Many times, while making home visits, people have hidden beer cans or pornographic materials upon my arrival. One pastor told me he encountered a man on the street that pulled a lit cigarette out of his mouth and put it in his pocket when they met. These are superficial, somewhat humorous examples, but they represent how people respond when they are convicted by the Spirit's presence in and through a believer.

The second reason people react negatively to your witness is the offense of the Cross. When you share the gospel, it sounds ridiculous to some who are confronted by its tenets. The gospel confounds modern convictions about self-esteem, self-righteousness, and self-sufficiency. It calls a person to abandon self-confidence and trust another person on life's most significant issue—eternal destiny. The message of the Cross is a "stumbling block" and "foolishness" (1 Corinthians 1:23) to some. Many are willing to follow Jesus the Teacher or Jesus the Healer. But receiving Jesus Christ Crucified is another matter. The Cross confronts our sin as its cause; our rebellion as its reason. Facing that ugly fact is painful.

Some people react to conviction of sin and confrontation by the Cross with bitterness and anger. They lash out at others, including Christians who witness to them, to deflect their guilt and shame.

This may manifest itself in ridicule or rejection, vitriolic debate or cutting words attacking the gospel . . . or you as its messenger. When this happens, despite your best efforts to prevent it, what should you do? How can you prepare yourself for these negative responses from others and steel yourself to continue sharing the gospel?

PLEASING GOD ABOVE ALL

The answer is found in Paul's final instructions to the Galatians when he addressed the issue of pleasing people as the source of relational tension about the gospel. He asked, "For am I now trying to win the favor of people, or God? Or am I striving to please people?" Then he continued, "If I were still trying to please people, I would not be a slave of Christ" (Galatians 1:10). The simple question is: Who are you ultimately trying to please? Will you do anything to have favor with people—to be liked? Or will you obey God—upholding the gospel even when doing so is unpopular or controversial?

Which is it for you? Have you made the decision to enjoy God's approval—or seek the favor of people? Settling this issue determines how you will respond to the relational tension that comes with sharing the gospel. When your ultimate goal is to be well liked, you will either avoid sharing the gospel or compromise it to make it more palatable. When your ultimate goal is favor with God, you will share the gospel and bear the consequences—whatever they may be. Resolving this issue is deeper than a simple commitment prayer. Getting to the root of this problem requires you to answer one of life's most important questions: Who or what makes you feel secure?

Most people answer this question from one of two broad categories—relationships or achievements. Workaholics believe if they do enough—sometimes even enough ministry—they will earn God's love and feel good about themselves. Their security comes from checking off their list and finding value in achieving. People pleasers, on the other hand, find their security in relationships. If everyone likes them, they like themselves. Anything that threatens relational peace must be avoided. Their security comes from feeling loved by people and loving them in return. Drinking from either of these wells for security—achievements or relationships—only satisfies for a short time. We need a more soul-quenching source.

Every Christian has the opportunity to live securely in relationship with God and find real security only in Him. The security of the believer isn't just about heaven; it's about life right now. If you are a follower of Jesus, you are as secure now as you will ever be. You have security as a believer. It's something you have, not something you get when you die. Jesus said: "My sheep hear My voice, I know them, and they follow Me. I give them eternal life, and they will never perish—ever! No one will snatch them out of My hand. My Father, who has given them to Me, is greater than all. No one is able to snatch them out of the Father's hand. The Father and I are one" (John 10:27–30).

Jesus promised security, now and later. He used the "two hands example"—a two-fisted grip illustrating you are doubly secured. Both Jesus and His Father have hold of you.

Your security as a believer means no one can harm you. No critical opinion defines you. No conflict threatens you. No other person, no matter how intense their negative response to the gospel, damages your confidence or credibility. Even if opposition moves beyond mere words to violence or martyrdom (as it already does in many places in the world), you are secure and will be secure. Your life—up to and including death—is eternally secure in Jesus.

Living out your commitment to share the gospel is beyond your strength or ability. You need help to stay on message. Fortunately, Jesus promised (John 16:7) and fulfilled His promise (Acts 1:8) to send the Holy Spirit to empower us to tell His story. Christians must trust the Spirit for guidance, motivation, and wisdom during conversations about the gospel. How does this work? Turn the page and let's discover new insights into trusting the Spirit for sharing the gospel more powerfully.

CHAPTER 4

EXPERIENCING
SPIRITUAL POWER

S HARING THE GOSPEL REQUIRES spiritual strength you can't generate by human effort. No matter how committed you are, you can't manufacture the power needed for evangelistic success. You lack sufficient spirituality to engage unbelievers with the gospel, present the plan of salvation in a way it makes sense, convince lost people of their need for Jesus, or regenerate sinners. If you try to do all this on your own—while life happens in unscripted conversations—you are headed for an emotional and spiritual meltdown. It can't be done. You are powerless to achieve spiritual results or supernatural outcomes. You don't even have a little power to improve by cultivating it. You are powerless. Without outside help, you won't be able to lead other people to faith in Jesus. It simply can't be done.

Thankfully, Jesus provides the power you need to success-fully live for Him and share His gospel. He promised, "I will ask the Father, and He will give you another Counselor to be with you forever. He is the Spirit of truth" (John 14:16), and "You will receive power when the Holy Spirit has come upon you, and you will be

My witness" (Acts 1:8). Jesus' promises were fulfilled when the Holy Spirit indwelled the church on the Day of Pentecost (Acts 2:1–4). The same power is now available to every believer (Romans 8:14–16). To cooperate with the Holy Spirit in sharing the gospel—to access His power for this important role—you must understand the scope of His work related to personal evangelism. He is involved in all aspects of communicating the gospel—from before you start to after you finish delivering the message.

THE HOLY SPIRIT WORKS WITH UNBELIEVERS

Too often, we assume the Holy Spirit begins working with unsaved people when we become concerned about them, when they attend a worship service, or when they are otherwise connected to some ministry project or program. This isn't the case. The Holy Spirit is always active among unbelievers, engaging them even when they aren't aware of His efforts.

The Holy Spirit prepares people to hear the gospel. Missionaries often report, upon sharing the gospel among those who had never heard it, that people have been prepared to hear it—sometimes by unusual means. These might include dreams, visions, predictions by community leaders, or prophecies passed down about teachers who would tell their people about an unknown God. When you witness, you will discover people are often open to the gospel, even where you live. They have been readied by God-shaped circumstances conspiring to prepare them to hear it. In the Bible, a Roman soldier's conversion illustrates how this process unfolds:

> *There was a man in Caesarea named Cornelius, a centurion of what was called the Italian Regiment. He was a devout man and feared God along with his whole household. He did many charitable deeds for the Jewish people and always prayed to God. At about three in the afternoon he distinctly saw in a vision an angel of God* (ACTS 10:1–3).

For Cornelius, a combination of spiritual interest ("prayed to God"), personal relationships ("did many charitable deeds for the Jewish people"), respect for God ("he was a devout man and feared God"), concern for his family ("feared God along with his whole household"), and spiritual prompting ("saw in a vision an angel") made him receptive to the gospel. When Peter witnessed to him, Cornelius received the gospel and publicly declared his faith through baptism (Acts 10:47–48). God is still at work, preparing people today to hear the gospel through many of the same means.

Kim was a single mom struggling to find her way in life. She enrolled her daughter in a church-sponsored child-care center, found a job, and prayed for God's help. Her little girl thrived in the supportive, stable environment at the preschool. Kim soon found herself lingering when she picked up her daughter, making friends with the teachers and director who ran the program. The workers' love for her child, their patience with Kim as a young mother learning to be a good parent, and their genuine concern for her well-being opened her heart to the gospel. After a few months, she attended church with one of the teachers. Shortly thereafter, the preschool's director led her to faith in Jesus.

Orville and Pearl were struggling with health challenges, one afraid of dying and the other afraid of living alone. Both were worried about their future. A friend, Avery, made a casual comment about his church, which piqued their interest. They expressed, although they had lived for seven decades without attending church, a desire to go to church with him. After attending for a few weeks, they committed themselves to Jesus by praying with Avery in their home. Aging, loss of health, fear of the future, and the casual comment of a friend all came together to crystallize their openness to the gospel.

Glen was an over-the-road trucker. He was driving alone, reflecting on his failures as a father, when in his words, "God got inside my truck." Glen had a profound sense of God's presence, conviction about past sins, and his need for radical changes in his lifestyle. A few days later, he attended a church service, heard the gospel, and committed himself to Jesus. His conversion changed his attitude and rekindled his relationships with his children. Within weeks, Glen's new life prompted his children to seek salvation through Jesus Christ.

These are examples of how the Holy Spirit prepares people to receive the gospel. He uses life crises, meaningful relationships, kind deeds, worship services, changes in other people, dramatic revelations, and countless other means to create an awareness of the need for salvation. The Holy Spirit orchestrates a symphony of circumstances, building to a crescendo of readiness to receive the gospel. He is always at work in the lives of people around us. Our challenge is discerning His activity and speaking the gospel in the best way at the opportune time.

The Holy Spirit convicts people of sin. One of the stark realities of humankind's spiritual condition is our sinfulness. The Bible says, "All have sinned and fall short of the glory of God" (Romans 3:23). Some deny this, claiming humans are essentially good. It's hard to hold that position if you have ever parented a two-year-old. More seriously, it isn't reasonable to believe people are essentially good in the face of human-initiated atrocities like genocide and infanticide. The evidence is overwhelming to any honest observer. We are all sinners. Jesus said the Holy Spirit would:

> *Convict the world about sin, righteousness, and judgment: About sin, because they do not believe in Me; about righteousness, because I am going to the Father and you will no longer see Me; and about judgment, because the ruler of this world has been judged* (JOHN 16:8–11).

Convicting sinners of their sin, their need for righteousness, and coming judgment is a primary function of the Holy Spirit. Underline this: convicting sinners is the Spirit's responsibility, not yours. Some Christians mistakenly think "real witnessing" is telling people how bad they are and how much judgment they deserve. Not so! Sharing the gospel is spreading good news. Establishing "all have sinned" sets the stage for the rest of the story—but it isn't the main narrative. The emphasis isn't on how bad we have been, but how good God is to love us anyway. Maintaining convictions and calling sin what it is, requires courage. But avoid being judgmental or legalistic toward others. Confronting people about their sin is heartrending and should evoke empathy and brokenness in us, not haughty satisfaction we have "straightened out another one." God help you if this is your attitude toward sinners!

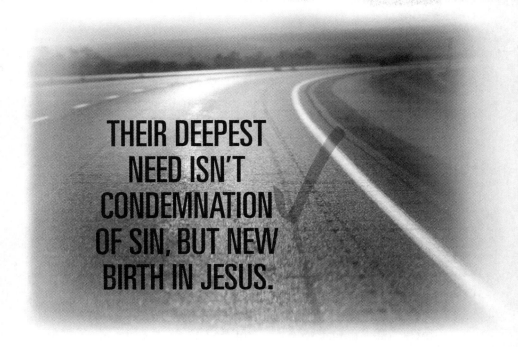

THEIR DEEPEST NEED ISN'T CONDEMNATION OF SIN, BUT NEW BIRTH IN JESUS.

Loving a sinful person means looking past his or her present behavior to the real need for life change through Jesus. When you befriend a lesbian couple, for example, it may be hard to focus on their need for salvation rather than their sexual behavior. But whether a person is a homosexual, adulterer, or pornographer—their deepest need isn't condemnation of their sexual sin, but new birth in Jesus. Irresponsible parents, arrogant teenagers, and crabby old men are hard to be around, unless you look beyond their presenting behavior to their deepest need—conversion. Loving sinners often involves tolerating offensive behavior and lousy attitudes—in short, caring for people in spite of their actions. These relationships can be draining but are necessary to stay connected with people who need the gospel.

While you are doing your part, the Holy Spirit is also doing His. He convicts concerning sin, righteousness, and judgment to come. The Spirit's conviction produces shame, guilt, and inner frustration. These weighty negative emotions demand resolution. People medicate (legally and illegally), abuse alcohol, overeat, pursue sexual fantasies, lash out in anger, or pursue other coping strategies in search of relief from the Spirit's conviction. As a witness, you have good news about the only legitimate means to resolving the resulting inner turmoil—forgiveness of sin through Jesus Christ.

Troy was a sex addict. Because of an abusive childhood, he had a very poor self-image and craved acceptance and intimacy. He pursued those goals by conquering women—one after another, sometimes changing partners multiple times each week. His resulting guilt was overwhelming and created a cause-and-effect downward spiral—loneliness, sex, guilt, inner condemnation, desperation for intimacy, more sex—and then the cycle repeated itself. Most of his friends were disgusted by his relational shallowness and vulgarity with women. One friend, however, saw his behavior as symptomatic rather than causal. He told Troy about the forgiveness Jesus offered, the inner healing He could provide, and intimacy achievable by basing relationships on His teachings. Troy's conversion liberated him from destructive life patterns by healing his deepest wounds.

Your unsaved friends and family, work associates, recreation partners, and strangers you encounter every day are all—at one level or another—being convicted of their sin by the Holy Spirit. As Spirit-managed circumstances intensify conviction, your response is vital. Your role is recognizing conviction of sin as it occurs, helping a person understand what is happening to them, and sharing the gospel as the means for resolving their dilemma.

The Holy Spirit accomplishes regeneration. One pressure point for Christians is fear they won't be able to convince non-Christians to believe the gospel. Well, you're right. You can't convince anyone to believe the gospel. Neither can you save anyone, cause their conversion, nor accomplish their regeneration. While you may assist with the delivery, the rest of the new birth experience is otherwise out of your hands.

Part of the Holy Spirit's work during a witnessing encounter is convincing an unbeliever of the truthfulness of the gospel. The words *convicting* and *convincing* are closely related. When you share the gospel, conviction of sin morphs into convincing of the truth about the gospel. In other words, while you communicate the gospel "head-to-head" (by sharing information about the death, burial, and resurrection of Jesus), the Spirit is convincing the person "heart-to-heart." A spiritual transformation is taking place, which you can't produce, control, manipulate, or assist.

Two theological extremes related to the Holy Spirit's work in conversion must be avoided. On one end of the spectrum are those who claim evangelism is entirely the Spirit's responsibility. He converts those He will, so witnessing is superfluous. Another group claims the opposite—only people who hear the gospel, pray a specific prayer, and commit themselves exactly according to a prescribed pattern are saved. Neither of these extremes—or their cousins in various religious disguises—captures the mystery of what actually happens during regeneration.

The new birth experience requires two things—a gospel presentation communicating salvation's availability through Jesus and God's grace regenerating new believers. Both are essential. Neither minimizes nor disqualifies the importance of the other. When they happen, they are complementary and produce amazing results.

Trish was an attractive socialite with two young children. Her husband was a prominent community leader. They had good friends, a Christian couple who were members of the same country club. Over time, these couples conversed about the gospel and their perspectives on God, church, and Christian service. Trish and her husband were God-fearers, occasional churchgoers with a positive view of Christianity. As Trish learned more about the gospel from her friends and observed the genuineness of their commitment, she became more concerned about her lack of a personal relationship with God. For her, church was a social obligation and Christianity a religious system. She wanted more.

Trish perceived me, a pastor, as a religious expert so she came to my office to discuss her faith questions. My approach was to share the gospel—simply, directly, and without any mention of church or religious obligations attached. Trish responded openly, and when asked if she was ready to commit her life to Jesus, she nodded yes. We bowed our heads and I instructed her to pray after me—not necessarily repeating my prayer verbatim but saying in her own words the thoughts expressed in my suggested prayer. Trish committed her life to Jesus Christ in a heartfelt prayer.

When she said amen, Trish lifted her head with a start. She put both hands over her heart and looked at me wide-eyed. Her face was flushed and tears were brimming in both eyes as she said, "Oh, this must be what it feels like to be born again!" We had not used the phrase *born again* in our conversation. Yet, somehow she knew it had just happened. This was the first and so far only time anyone has ever made a commitment to Jesus in my presence and then provided such succinct, spontaneous commentary on the experience. Trish was born again, regenerated by the Holy Spirit, as promised: "He saved us—not by works of righteousness that we had done but according to His mercy, through the washing of regeneration and renewal by the Holy Spirit" (Titus 3:5).

THE HOLY SPIRIT WORKS THROUGH BELIEVERS

While the Holy Spirit prepares unbelievers for the gospel, convicts them of sin, convinces them of truth, and accomplishes their conversion—the Spirit also works through believers in the witnessing process. You aren't alone in your mission to share the gospel. Jesus promised you a Companion (John 16:7), and the Holy Spirit is now ever-present with you (2 Corinthians 1:22). The Spirit has many functions and responsibilities with and through believers, but during gospel-sharing efforts he is particularly active. Here are some key ways the Holy Spirit works during a witnessing encounter.

The Holy Spirit empowers believers. Are you afraid to share your faith? Join the club! Most believers struggle with fear of failure, ridicule, embarrassment, or some other inadequacy in telling others about Jesus. Fear is an obstacle to overcome, not an excuse for neglecting your responsibility. Spiritual power produces the courage needed to communicate the gospel.

Jesus promised, "You will receive power when the Holy Spirit has come upon you" (Acts 1:8). The initial manifestation of the Holy Spirit in the church was on Pentecost (Acts 2:1–4). Paul later assured all believers that subsequent to Pentecost they had received the Spirit at conversion: "The Spirit himself testifies together with our spirit that we are God's children" (Romans 8:16). He later described every believer as "a sanctuary of the Holy Spirit who is in you" (1 Corinthians 6:19). In summary, every believer receives the Holy Spirit at conversion and is permanently indwelled by the Spirit from that moment forward. A different experience, the filling of the Holy Spirit, will be discussed later in this chapter. For now, focus on these two realities—you received the Spirit at conversion and the Spirit is now a permanent presence in your life.

Since this is true, the Holy Spirit's power for witnessing is latent in you all the time. How do you activate that power? The answer:

by faith. Experienced witnesses know the Holy Spirit's power is actuated during a witnessing encounter—not before. It's futile to pray for spiritual power, waiting for a holy buzz or spine-tingling urge to settle on you, before you try to witness. Instead, trust the Spirit's power to be evident in the moment and start sharing the gospel. When you do this, you will discover spiritual power is accessed by stepping forward in faith. Step out boldly, trusting that the Spirit's power will sustain you.

Long ago, God's people were on a trek from Egypt to their new land in Israel. They arrived at the Jordan River but were stymied how to cross it since it was at flood stage. Their leader, Joshua, instructed priests to carry the ark of the covenant to the front of the procession. He told the people, "When the feet of the priests who carry the ark of the Lord, the Lord of all the earth, come to rest in the Jordan's waters, its waters will be cut off " (Joshua 3:13). As the priests carrying the ark walked forward, their sandal-shod feet landed on dry ground. This story illustrates the timeliness of God's power at work through His people. God works in the moment, not before or after. The river dried up as their feet stepped forward. So it is with speaking the gospel. Before you start, you may feel afraid—powerless for the task. But as you speak, the Spirit energizes you for the encounter. The Holy Spirit provides the power for witnessing. You access that power by sharing the gospel and trusting Him to intervene just when you need it.

The Holy Spirit gives authority to believers. A related concept to spiritual power is spiritual authority. Jesus claimed all authority belonged to Him, yet He shares it with His followers for kingdom purposes (Matthew 28:18–20). While the Spirit empowers witnesses, Jesus' name and the gospel's truth have their own authority. When you speak in the name of Jesus, you speak with authority about the Source of salvation. When you share the gospel, you are speaking inherently powerful truth. Both the name of Jesus (encompassing His life, death, burial, resurrection, and ascension) and the gospel (the good news of salvation) are messages with authority—in and of themselves without any human additions. This is important because of the impotence we often feel when sharing our faith with people who are older, more mature, better educated, or more successful than we perceive ourselves to be.

A group of women jokingly and affectionately named (by me, not them) the Country Club Bible Study was quite intimidating. They were the leading women of our community. Their husbands had positions of influence, all had significant financial resources, all had beautiful homes, all traveled extensively, and all were well-educated (some formally, all by enriching life experiences). My role: spiritual adviser and consultant about questions emerging from their weekly gatherings. Some were Christians, some only curious seekers. From time to time, they invited me to meet with them. While they were always gracious, the questions were pointed and earnest. Sometimes, the answers were difficult—confronting their attitudes and behaviors in uncomfortable ways. This was compounded by an inescapable reality: I was young enough to be their son. My task was also clear: give good answers to their questions based on scriptural insights and perspectives. My authority was not my age (too young), my experiences (too green), or my achievements (too few). My authority came from confidence in Jesus, the Word of God, and the gospel. Sharing answers based on those sources gave me significant influence in a group that normally would have considered my input novice, even

WHEN YOU SPEAK THE GOSPEL, TRUST THE SPIRIT TO HELP YOU.

juvenile. Speaking with authority is more about your message than you as a messenger. When you speak the gospel, you speak truth with its own authenticating authority.

The Holy Spirit gives wisdom to believers. When you dialogue with people about the gospel, puzzling questions and difficult issues can arise. Some Christians avoid these discussions because they are afraid they won't have all the answers. Relax, you won't. But that doesn't mean you should avoid unscripted conversations about the gospel. The Holy Spirit illuminates us, helping us respond in situations for which little preparation is possible. It's impossible to read enough books, memorize enough answers, or research enough issues to be thoroughly versed on every possible objection or question about the gospel. Instead, focus on communicating the gospel and trusting the Holy Spirit to help you know what to say in the moment.

Jesus told the disciples:

> *Whenever they bring you before synagogues and rulers and authorities, don't worry about how you should defend yourselves or what you should say. For the Holy Spirit will teach you at that very hour what must be said* (LUKE 12:11–12).

While that promise was to disciples launching an early preaching tour, the principle is also applicable for you. When you speak the gospel, trust the Spirit to help you know what to say, when to say it, and how to say it. Trust the Spirit for discernment about a person's genuine needs, underlying concerns, and past experiences prompting their questions or motivating their resistance. Sometimes, answering questions by genuine seekers is helpful. Other times, it's necessary to see through superfluous questions and probe for a deeper issue. Spiritual discernment is required to know the difference.

Jackson's wife, Beth, was intrigued by the gospel and considering committing herself to Jesus. After several conversations with Beth and Jackson, it was obvious he was also interested in the gospel but had many reservations. He called me and said, "I have several questions about Christianity and religion. Can you come over tonight and answer them?" When I arrived, he pulled a piano bench between our two chairs, unfolded his list of 17 questions, and started with number one: "Who is God and how do you know He exists?" Nothing like starting with a softball!

No amount of preparation or advance study could have prepared me for his list. It was a convoluted collection of spiritual questions mainly designed to mask Jackson's real issue—he didn't want the conversation to get too personal, exposing his insecurities and fears about the future. As long as we discussed Christianity objectively, he felt safe. After we finished question 17 (and I can't remember my response to any of the questions), I asked, "Now, may I ask you one question?" Jackson agreed and I asked, "Are you ready to have a personal, not a theoretical conversation about Jesus Christ?" He said he was and for the next hour we discussed the gospel and the possibility of his making a personal commitment to Jesus. Some weeks later, he decided to become a Christian.

My answers that night may have contributed to Jackson's conversion, but they were not the primary factor. The Spirit helped me give simple, direct answers to his questions—followed by a clear and personal presentation of the gospel. No person has ever been argued or debated into the kingdom of God. Don't stress about being able to win arguments or convince skeptics about the gospel. Focus your energy on maintaining a loving attitude, making a clear gospel presentation, and trusting the Spirit for wisdom to handle issues as they arise. The Holy Spirit works through willing Christians. He gives you power, authority, and wisdom. The pressing question, then, is How do you intensify your experience of the Spirit's power?

EXPERIENCING THE HOLY SPIRIT

Since you received the Holy Spirit at your conversion and have been indwelled continuously since that moment, your goal isn't getting more of the Spirit. Your challenge is experiencing the Spirit—learning to sense His leadings and submit to His promptings. In biblical language, you must be "filled with the Spirit" (Ephesians 5:18). Being filled with the Spirit means you are controlled, directed, or guided by the Spirit. It's the day-by-day experience of the Holy Spirit's supremacy. Specifically, how does this happen?

There's no biblical formula for being filled with the Holy Spirit. In God's wisdom, the Bible describes *aspects* and *results* of being filled, but never lists *steps* guaranteeing the experience. Given our tendency toward legalism, this benefits us. If God had established such a formula, we would have probably turned it into a 40-day program with an acronym for a title. Programmatic steps to spiritual power are impossible. One concept completely contradicts the other. We are not, however, left without counsel about being filled with the Spirit. Let's consider several aspects (not steps) of this spiritual process outlined in the Bible.

The first aspect of being filled with the Holy Spirit is your conversion. All believers:

> *Led by God's Spirit are God's sons. For you did not receive a spirit of slavery to fall back into fear, but you received the Spirit of adoption, by whom we cry out, "Abba, Father!" The Spirit Himself testifies together with our spirit that we are God's children* (ROMANS 8:14–16).

As a Christian, at your conversion, you received the Holy Spirit as a permanent, indwelling presence. If you are a Christian, you are indwelled by the Spirit and have the capacity to be filled with the Spirit. This is your present and constant spiritual condition.

The second aspect of being filled with the Spirit is surrendering control of your life (Ephesians 5:18). Remember, the words *influenced* or *controlled* are synonyms for the biblical word translated "filled." Many years ago a deacon told me being Spirit-filled required "acquiescence to the heart to God." *Acquiescence* was a new word for me. It means "passive submission, willing compliance." Being filled with the Spirit involves surrendering yourself to the Spirit's control. It's an intentional, willing choice to passively submit—to acquiesce—to the Spirit's influence.

While submission can be expressed in many ways, perhaps the simplest is through regular prayer—submitting your will to the Spirit's control and asking for His filling. Fervent, transparent prayer crystallizes submission. Formulaic prayers mumbled habitually are insufficient. Crying out to God—earnestly, passionately, abandoning all pretenses—genuinely reveals lack of self-trust and a longing for the Spirit's filling. Praying this way reveals a holy desperation to experience the Holy Spirit's power.

This doesn't imply strenuous effort makes your prayers more effective. Sincere prayer expresses your submission to God. But there's no magic in bowing, kneeling, weeping, or crying out to God. No outer work, no matter how earnest, produces spiritual power. The issue is *acquiescence* of your heart, not any certain prayer method. Outward expressions in prayer are helpful when they symbolize your innermost desires. They can also facilitate humbling yourself, assuring you of God's favor because He "resists the proud, but gives grace to the humble" (1 Peter 5:5). But remember, no outer work accomplishes inner surrender. That's done by a choice to submit your will to the Spirit's control.

A third aspect of being filled with the Spirit is confessing sin and stopping sinful behavior. Since the Holy Spirit entered your life at conversion, being filled with the Spirit is more about removing barriers to His flow through you than obtaining something new. This idea is captured in the simple phrase, "Don't stifle the Spirit" (1 Thessalonians 5:19). Other translations use the word *quench* instead of *stifle*. Either word communicates the same idea. The Holy Spirit is alive in you. Yet, you have the capacity to stifle or quench His influence. How?

The Holy Spirit can be stifled or quenched—another related word is *grieved*—by your attitudes or behaviors. In the midst of instructions about proper behavior for believers, Paul wrote, "And don't grieve God's Holy Spirit" (Ephesians 4:30). That admonition is in the midst of instructions about managing anger, showing integrity at work, communicating with wholesome words, and avoiding bitterness, wrath, and slander. The placement of the warning is significant.

You can grieve, stifle, or quench the Holy Spirit's influence by your behaviors and attitudes. Your actions reveal who is controlling you. Your attitudes show who or what shapes your thinking. When you are in control, your choices drift toward self-serving, self-justifying behavior unseemly for believers. These actions reveal you aren't submitted to the Spirit; therefore, not filled with the Spirit. Your actions, and the attitudes motivating those actions, are a barometer on your spiritual condition.

A final aspect of being filled with the Holy Spirit is accepting His filling by faith. When you pray—confessing known sin, submitting yourself to the Spirit's control, and asking for the filling of the Spirit—no special feeling will necessarily wash over you. Giving control to the Spirit is a spiritual exercise accomplished by faith. Remember, "As you have received Christ Jesus the Lord, walk in Him" (Colossians 2:6). You received Jesus into your life by faith. In that moment, the Holy Spirit permanently indwelled you. Submitting yourself to the Spirit's control is a continuing act of faith. Believing you have His power is a faith-filled choice.

This has particular application when sharing the gospel. As we have already learned (from the illustration about crossing the river with the ark of the covenant), trusting the power of the Spirit requires you step forward by faith and begin to witness. Like those priests carrying the ark into the river, you count on God's power to be evident in the moment you speak the gospel. A gospel dialogue is a serendipitous, spontaneous coming together of a witnessing believer, an authoritative message, the Holy Spirit's power, and a receptive unbeliever. During those conversations, when you are filled with the Spirit, you may feel like you are on holy ground with a sense of awe, mystery, and humility at being allowed to participate in eternity-shaping events. It's a spiritual high you can't replicate any other way.

Gerald was learning how to share his faith. We visited a man in his home who was ready to believe the gospel and receive Jesus as his Savior and Lord. His conversion was emotional—the heartfelt trans-formation of a rough-and-tough man ready for a new start. Gerald witnessed his first new birth! He felt the Spirit's power in his witness and saw the Spirit's work of regeneration. As we left the house, he bounded down the front steps and said, "That was awesome! Let's go find another one!"

Let's go find another one! Maybe for you it will be your first one. Whether you are a novice witness or a veteran who shares her faith often, you will be awed by the Spirit's power working through you and with you while you share the gospel. Experiencing the Spirit's power in these encounters never grows routine or boring. Spiritual life is *life*—vibrant, ever-changing, unpredictable, and unscripted. Living this way is more satisfying than a fine meal. Like Jesus told His disciples after talking with the woman at the well, witnessing Christians have "food to eat that you don't know about" (John 4:32).

What a satisfying feast it is!

The foundational spiritual tripod for a witnessing lifestyle is prayer, the gospel, and the Holy Spirit. Establish these basics as you reshape your life toward more intentionally conversing with others about Jesus. Getting more intentional in these efforts is the focus in the next section of the book. But remember, techniques and approaches are only useful when they rest on the right spiritual foundation. Do whatever it takes to stabilize your commitment to prayer, understanding of the gospel, and experience with the Holy Spirit's power. Then you will be ready to improve your witnessing skill set for more meaningful conversations about Jesus. Let's turn our attention toward that goal in the next few chapters.

**LIFESTYLE CHOICES
FOR SHARING
THE GOSPEL
AS LIFE HAPPENS**

CHAPTER 5

REACHING YOUR FRIENDS AND FAMILY WITH THE GOSPEL

I N THE CATEGORY of Dumb Things Pastors Say, one of my favorites is: "We need to get outside the walls of the church." Before lambasting other pastors, I confess I said this more than once (OK, a lot of times) when I was a pastor. One day it dawned on me most church members spend almost all their time "outside the walls" of their church. They work at secular companies, go to public schools, do workouts at community centers, and relax with friends from all those venues. Most Christians, like you, are already well connected outside the walls of the church.

When pastors implore their members to go "outside the walls," what they usually mean is participation in a church-sponsored out-reach program or ministry activity. These range from door-to-door visitation programs to servant evangelism projects (like commu-nity cleanup days or operating crisis pregnancy centers). These are worthwhile approaches to energizing and organizing believers to interact with their community. Nothing in this chapter should be construed as opposing any type of church-based, programmatic strategy for reaching out to unbelievers. These approaches are viable avenues for sharing the gospel, training believers to witness more effectively, focusing the resources of a church on a particular community problem, and mobilizing believers for evangelistic activity.

This chapter, however, is *not* about those kinds of projects. It's about you strengthening relationships with unbelievers you already know. It's about developing those relationships toward the goal of sharing Jesus with your friends and family members. It's also about building new relationships by engaging people with the gospel who share an interest or activity with you. Your most fertile field for the gospel is people you already see on a regular basis in your normal life patterns—work, school, neighborhood, and so forth. If this is true, what can you do to become more effective in sharing the gospel as life happens?

DEPLOYED, NOT DISPERSED

Start with a new perspective: you are deployed, not just dispersed, in your community. What's the difference? When away from church or Christian fellowship, many believers consider themselves dispersed. They are scattered among unsaved people—at work, school, or in social settings—but keep those relationships casual to avoid contamination with worldly behavior. These Christians are overly concerned about being tainted by their environment, too insecure to maintain their convictions while interfacing with unbelievers.

There is a clear biblical warning to "keep oneself unstained by the world" (James 1:27). Without question, you must pursue purity and avoid behavior outside biblical parameters. But many Christians misinterpret this verse to mean "keep oneself away from any meaningful contact with people in the world who engage in sinful behavior." Believers who think this way are dispersed—away from their Christian cocoon and not comfortable until they get back in it. An enabling by-product of this mind-set is the proliferation of church-sponsored activities—from sports teams to coffee shops to book clubs—that keep Christians clustered with their believing (and therefore, "safe") friends most of the time. Dispersed Christians don't feel comfortable "out there" alone. They huddle with other believers as often as possible. You can't live like that if you are serious about engaging people with the gospel.

You must think of yourself as deployed—not dispersed. While you still recognize your church and Christian friends as home base, you are comfortable going out from them to engage unbelievers. When a military unit is sent into combat, they don't wander around looking for interesting things to see or do. They are on a mission, usually narrowly defined with results specifically measured. They are deployed, not dispersed; sent on a mission, not scattered to the winds. They ship out, accomplish a specific purpose, and return home (only to repeat the process until the ultimate objective is reached). A deployed Christian has a similar mind-set. You leave the safety and comfort of Christian community, communicate the gospel in your circle of influence or interest, and gather with believers from time to time to recharge for future service. You then repeat this process for as long as God gives you continued opportunity to serve Him.

When you are deployed, the people in your daily life become your missions field. You already live among the people you are responsible to reach with the gospel. This is a staggering revelation for many Christians who think of their daily life (work, school, etc.) and their ministry life (church attendance, outreach projects, etc.) as two separate spheres—in parallel orbits never intended to intersect. Consider this scenario: You accept a visitation assignment from your church. You knock on a stranger's door and ask the man who answers if you can talk with him and his family about Jesus. He says yes. You enter and meet his wife—who works in the cubicle next to yours. She comments, "I didn't know you were a Christian or went to a church in our area." That seems absurd—yet it's the way many Christians live. Evangelism is what you do among strangers on outreach night, not friends who work in an adjacent office. Witnessing is confined to a church program, not embraced as a personal privilege. Deployed Christians, however, reject this dichotomy and live their mission of sharing the gospel all the time.

DEPLOYED: SOME PRACTICAL HELP

Jesus modeled a deployed lifestyle. He left heaven—that's really leaving home base—to live among people. He talked with, prayed for, cried with, and touched countless individuals. Jesus showed up in all kinds of places—from synagogues to water wells to private homes to fishing boats. Jesus attended weddings, funerals, dinner parties, and other gatherings of family and friends. He taught people how to become His disciples as a natural part of daily interactions with them. How can you be more like Jesus in this regard? After three decades of practicing, plus watching others do this effectively, here are some practical keys to having a more intentional gospel awareness of people around you. Do these things if you want to develop a deployed mind-set as a believer on a mission.

Be engaged. When you are with people, are you really *with* them? Or, are people around you part of the wallpaper? Do you even notice them? Are you distracted by other tasks or priorities? If so, make the choice to turn off your cell phone and declutter your calendar so you can focus on genuinely connecting with people.

One man heard me teach on reaching friends with the gospel and was particularly intrigued by our family's outreach through youth sports. While our children were growing up, all three played multiple sports. We were always on the way to or from some practice or game year-round. Young athletes tend to play multiple sports with the same other youngsters so we were frequently with the same parents at practices, games, team parties, and fund-raisers. We didn't need a visitation program to spend our evenings with lost people; we were with them multiple nights every week. Over the years, we were intentional about engaging these friends with the gospel. Several of them have become Christians—by far the most rewarding part of our family's sports lifestyle.

Inspired by our story, this fellow told me, "That really works for you. I'm also heavily involved in youth sports but don't seem to have the same opportunities to share the gospel you do." We talked about his situation, but I had no real solutions for him. A few weeks later, however, we happened to be at a game where our children were playing against each other. During the game, I talked with various parents/friends—catching up on their families, talking about problems at work, laughing at the funny things happening on the field, and following up on past conversations (like updates on sick parents, etc.). My friend spent the entire game on his cell phone. He made call after call, no doubt doing something more important than engaging the people watching the game. His problem was simple: he was at

PRIORITIZE BUILDING RELATIONSHIPS WITH UNBELIEVERS.

the game, but not really *at the game*. His thoughts, focus, and energy were someplace else.

Choosing to make phone calls or to watch every riveting minute of a child's ball game isn't the point. The problem is lack of engagement—of not really being there. When you are deployed with the gospel, you remind yourself before you get out of the car, *I am about to enter my missions field. I must be at my best. I must engage people fully. I have a purpose for being here—making friends, showing the love of Jesus, and sharing the gospel (or as much of the gospel as possible).* Learn to really connect with people and prioritize building relationships with unbelievers—not just being in their general vicinity and hoping for the best.

Be persistent. Some advocates for lifestyle evangelism leave the impression every conversation is an in-depth discussion of the gospel and someone is being saved almost every week. That may be true for someone, but it isn't true for most of us. Many relationships mature over time, slowly building to the place where the gospel can be shared appropriately. Even then, it's not always immediately embraced. Some witnessing relationships last for years with intermittent conversations about the gospel. We have friends who have been open to the gospel from almost the first time we met (some even asking us to share it with them). We also have friends we have prayed for and cared for without much response—yet. Sadly, we have also made mistakes by awkwardly or prematurely introducing the gospel into a relationship.

Soon after we moved to Oregon to plant a new church, we met Stan and Laura through coaching youth sports. Stan and I signed up to coach, got paired up, and had a fun season together. At the end of the year, they invited our family to their home for an end-of-season cookout celebrating surviving the T-ball season. It was a great night, until my mindless insensitivity almost ruined everything.

After dinner, Laura asked me, "So why did you guys move to Oregon? Something about a church, right?" This was my opening! I poured out all the reasons we had moved to Oregon, including our desire to evangelize unbelievers in the Northwest (one of the most unchurched regions in the United States). Something about my attitude piqued Laura who replied, "So you came out here to Oregon to save all us stupid pagans, right?" Not exactly! Backpedaling fast, I tried to explain my comments only to discover the old saying is true: "You can't dig yourself out of a hole." Oh, how I wish life had been more scripted that night! I apologized for my slight to her regional pride, as well as my judgmental spirit. She waved it off saying, "No big deal." We left that night wondering if we would ever talk with them again. We did, and ultimately became good friends.

Over the years, we have maintained a strong relationship with this family. We have shared ball games, family gatherings, weddings, and funerals with them. We have continued to be friends, persistently praying and talking about the gospel for more than 20 years. Sharing the gospel in personal relationships requires persistence. When you share with a stranger you may never see again, you just move on and pray for the best. When you engage good friends with the gospel who aren't ready to receive it, your response is crucial. You must patiently preserve the relationship and stay friends even if they are slow to respond to the gospel.

Be sensitive. Knowing when to share the gospel (or even part of it) and when to ask a person to commit to Jesus requires spiritual sensitivity. There are times when your witness may not be well received or it isn't the best time to share the gospel. For example, when you are at work, you should be working, not undermining your integrity by wasting company time. Save the witnessing for breaks or when your shift ends. When a person is in a public place, it's usually not a good idea to put them on the spot about something as personal as their salvation. While the gospel can be introduced in most any conversational setting, it's often best to ask for a more private meeting to discuss it thoroughly. Fully sharing the plan of salvation and asking for a commitment is usually best accomplished when a friend or family member is able to respond without distraction.

Alan is a friend who umpired with me for several years. Over time, I learned about different facets of his life—military service, health concerns, troubled relationships, and his praying grandmother. But, frankly, we mostly talked umpiring. We enjoyed umpiring as partners but were seldom together away from the ballpark. My mentoring advanced his umpiring career and helped him get his first playoff tournament assignments. He was on the field with me for my worst umpiring moment ever (details not necessary, but I really blew it). We laughed about it later—and it turned into a bonding experience for us. When we moved from Oregon, I wanted Alan to hear the gospel from me before we left. He accepted my lunch invitation. I shared the gospel with him—away from the field and any distraction or embarrassment our conversation might have caused him in that setting.

Remember the earlier formula about open doors for the gospel—people die, health fails, relationships struggle, and things break. When your friends have any of these experiences, approach them gently and discern their openness to the gospel. Approach them on their terms, but let them know you care. One of the most powerful ways to communicate concern is to pray with or promise to pray for a hurting person. You may be so accustomed to prayer, and being prayed for, that you don't realize how moving "I'm praying for you" is to most people. Grown men get glassy-eyed when they hear those words. Actually praying with a hurting person can be even more powerful. These simple acts take many relationships to the next level and pave the way for future conversations about spiritual issues, including the gospel.

Being bold in your witness is a spiritual necessity (remember, it's one of the prayer requests described in chap. 2). Discerning an appropriate opportunity to share Jesus must never be an excuse to avoid witnessing. Don't hide behind "waiting for the right time" and never get around to communicating the gospel. Words like *usually, often*, and *most of the time*, have been used in this section to indicate waiting for an opportune time is important. This isn't, however, an absolute requirement making you so uncertain you never get around to sharing your faith. The gospel can be shared in almost any setting. My conversion occurred at a county fair, with hundreds of people milling past the booth where a church was telling people about Jesus.

Be bold, but avoid being crass, rude, or arrogant with your witness. Be intentional, but sensitive in the manner, location, and timing of a gospel presentation.

Be contagious. Do you enjoy life? Let it show! Sharing the gospel is a serious responsibility, not a joy-sucking burden. Jesus enjoyed being with people. He went to celebrations like weddings, banquets, and religious services. He went fishing and interacted with children. Jesus attracted people. We must follow His example. As a Christian, enjoy life and let your enthusiasm for your faith be

IT'S ABOUT
TAKING THE
GOSPEL WITH YOU.

contagious. People should catch the life-changing joy of the gospel just from being around you.

Living and sharing the gospel, however, isn't only for extroverted people. You don't have to be the life of the party to effectively show your faith. Authenticity, genuineness, and thoughtful compassion from a shy, reserved person can be as winsome as the spontaneous boldness of the brashest type-A personality. Being yourself, and expressing the gospel through your God-given personality, is better than faking a phony witness. A caricature is never better than the real thing. Authenticity is always attractive. Genuineness is seldom belittled.

Sharing the gospel in a comfortable way, in your natural surroundings, and in places and among people you enjoy is much easier than a forced witness in a contrived environment. What do you enjoy doing? Playing softball, volunteering at a library, watching NASCAR racing, attending a painting class? Who do enjoy being with? Cowboys, cheerleaders, performance artists, kayakers? Christians are found in almost every nook and cranny of our culture. We don't need to go there, we are already there. Getting busy sharing your faith isn't about abandoning things you enjoy so you can do more ministries. It's about taking the gospel with you, remembering you are deployed, as you live your faith among your family and friends.

Karen is a Civil War reenactment buff. She plays a surgeon, complete with the outfit and primitive medical tools as props. Hundreds of her friends gather periodically to reenact Civil War battles, relive part of the history of our country, and talk about the lessons learned from the conflict. She gives devotionals for the group based on spiritual thoughts recorded in diaries and letters of the actual participants. This leads, naturally, to follow-up conversations with her friends about the gospel and its implications for today.

Jim hunts, as do several men in his church and many men in his community. During elk season, Jim sets up a hunter's camp for two weeks. It's publicized in his small town as a place to gather for some company, coffee, and whatever is on the spit that night. Some men cycle through the camp, others come every night. It's well known in the area—not only for the food but also for the evening devotional. The organizers lead a no-pressure, you-all-come, unscripted discussion of God, the wonder of His creation, and fullness of His revelation in Jesus. Over the years, many men have placed faith in Jesus through this camp.

My mother, well past age 70, still goes on multiday trail rides with her riding club. They usually ride over a weekend, and one member of the group leads Cowboy Church on Sunday. According to my mom, everyone comes—even those "who would never darken the church doors." People who enjoy cowboy culture are more likely to listen to the gospel from a fellow trail-rider than anyone else.

When groups of people do something they enjoy, it's a natural expression of mutual friendship to share what's important to each person—including the gospel. Enjoy life. Be yourself. Make friends. Be a friend. Share the gospel in the most natural setting possible— among people who share your interests, passions, or activities. In those settings and among those relationships you will find the greatest receptivity to your witness.

After sharing the gospel with a businessman, he told me, "I understand what you're saying. But you're a pastor. If I ever accept Jesus, it will be with Mick. He's a businessman like me. We face the same pressures. I want to talk to him first." Thankfully, Mick was able to lead his friend to Jesus a few months later. People are usually most open to hearing the gospel from someone like them. That's why missionaries quickly want national believers to replace them as the leaders who share the gospel in other countries. The same principle works in various segments of our society. People like you are most likely to listen to you. Commonality facilitates credibility.

WHAT IF YOU DON'T HAVE MANY NON-CHRISTIAN FRIENDS?

The sad reality is many Christians, particularly church leaders or people who have been believers for many years, don't have many non-Christian friends. Do you? Do you know any unbelievers who are true friends—not just acquaintances? Do you go boating, attend a concert, or play dominoes with them? Do unbelievers call you when their car won't start, their plumbing breaks, they want to go fishing, or their kids need a place to stay so they can have a weekend away? If you don't have non-Christian friends like that, it's time to make some lifestyle adjustments.

The following statement may be controversial and easily misunderstood. As a mature Christian, in order to build relationships with unbelieving friends or family members, *you may need to attend fewer church activities.* The Bible says: "Let us be concerned about one another in order to promote love and good works, not staying away from our meetings, as some habitually do, but encouraging each other, and all the more as you see the day drawing near" (Hebrews 10:24–25).

This directive requires Christians to maintain fellowship with other believers. But it doesn't mean you must attend every function sponsored by your church. Every Christian must be an active member of a church—never falling into the habit of negligent absenteeism leading to spiritual aloofness. We all need to hear biblical preaching, participate in Bible study, humble ourselves through public worship, and draw strength from fellowship with other Christians. But, does this mean our entire schedule must orbit around church activities? The answer, if you plan to develop friendships with unbelievers, is no.

Some churches seem determined to extinguish opportunities for their members to have any contact with unsaved people. They sponsor church athletic leagues, open church-owned restaurants, develop church-based activities for every age and interest, and construct facilities to house all these programs. While token encouragement to "bring your non-Christian friends" is offered, for all practical purposes these activities are a "Christian alternative" to participating in the "worldly community." While positive motives drive these efforts, and some good comes from them, the unintended consequence is insulation from engaging lost people through sharing daily life with them. How can you change these patterns?

First, make a foundational decision that essential church participation is nonnegotiable. You can't use "being with my unsaved friends" as an excuse to violate the biblical mandate to maintain close connection with your church. Every believer, no matter how mature, needs continuing doses of preaching, worship, Bible study, and fellowship to stay strong. You must, however, balance these important churchcentric functions with a commitment to fulfill the evangelistic imperative of the church—reaching more people with the gospel.

Second, choose to invest time with unbelievers. This may be challenging for you, particularly if you have equated Christian fidelity with church attendance. When we started a church in Oregon, Stella was a young woman who had grown up as a pastor's daughter. She had always attended church several times a week—and, in her mind, her faithfulness to God was defined by that practice. Our church intentionally developed a streamlined schedule and kept expectations for being "at church" to a minimum. We challenged every member to stay connected (or get connected) to their community, develop witnessing relationships, and help grow our church by reaching friends in their networks. It was an adjustment for Stella, who wondered if she was compromising her commitment to the Lord by being a member of a church that defined discipleship by life transformation, not program participation. After a few months, however, she told me, "I am going to church less than any time in my life. But I am doing what the church is supposed to be doing better than ever!"

Third, change your attitude toward non-Christians and the time you invest in relationships with them. When people feel they are objects, prospects, or targets, they will *not* want to be friends with you. If unbelievers sense you are judgmental or condemnatory toward them, they will shut down any effort to deepen their friendship with you. Wise Christians learn to walk the tightrope of embracing sinners, while not approving sinful behavior. That sounds easy. It's not. When someone is having an affair, drinking to excess, gossiping about people in the office, watching pornography, neglecting their children, or abusing their spouse—it's hard to keep perspective and differentiate the sin from the sinner.

Among many men, for example, profanity is as common as breathing. Constantly hearing it can be wearisome, especially when Jesus and God are used as curse words. But profanity isn't the real problem—only a symptom of insecurity or immaturity. Twelve-year-old boys curse to try to prove their masculinity and gain approval by their peers. Men (and more and more women) do the same thing. But words aren't the problem. Solving the underlying issue—finding validation for life through Jesus—is the real need. Keeping the focus on a person's true needs, rather than presenting issues, requires spiritual maturity and emotional discipline.

Jesus modeled the importance of sticking to the main issue when He attended a dinner party with a collection of outcasts and rejects. Jesus had a disciple named Matthew, a former tax collector, which was a disdained occupation in the first century. Matthew's friends were tax collectors and other societal pariahs. One night, he invited Jesus over for dinner. The Bible describes the scene this way:

> *While He was reclining at the table in the house, many tax collectors and sinners came as guests to eat with Jesus and His disciples. When the Pharisees saw this, they asked His disciples, "Why does your Teacher eat with tax collectors and sinners?" But when He heard this, He said, "Those who are well don't need a doctor, but the sick do. Go and learn what this means: I desire mercy and not sacrifice. For I didn't come to call the righteous, but sinners* (MATTHEW 9:10–13).

When Jesus ate with sinners, notice who was offended—the Pharisees. The religious leaders were angry because He was breaking their rules by eating with sinners. Jesus reminded them He had come to save sinners, not congratulate the self-righteous. Jesus partied with sinners, kept the focus on their spiritual condition, and wasn't distracted from His mission by their behavior. Having table fellowship with sinners shows Jesus was comfortable with them, accepting of them, and friendly toward them. You must develop this same spiritual self-discipline—the ability to love and be loved by unbelievers, while keeping the focus on their need for salvation no matter how offensive their behavior. It's a lot easier to read that last sentence than to live it.

Dan frequently beat his wife. Mary came to me for counseling, bruises barely hidden by makeup and a high-neck sweater. Another Christian couple, Clint and Deana, had been consistently and patiently reaching out to Dan and Mary—telling them how Jesus could save them and restore their marriage. My anger toward Dan made it almost impossible for me to be involved. Dan didn't need Jesus, he needed Muhammad Ali in his prime to stop by and even the score! When someone is being abused, it's difficult to care about the abuser. Yet, in this case, Clint and Deana managed their emotions, kept the focus on the real problem (sin-induced insecurity and deeply rooted anger producing violent outbursts), and loved their friends through it all. After several interventions and multiple long nights, Dan finally submitted himself to Jesus as Savior and Lord. His healing started. The marriage took longer. Tolerating him, much less loving him through this process, was a significant challenge for all involved.

Finally, determine to speak the gospel to your friends and settle for nothing less as the culmination of your relationship with them. Some Christians claim, "My life is my witness." That's impossible! There's no biblical support for that claim. Your life choices support and validate your witness, not substitute for it. Jesus said, "By this all people will know that you are My disciples, if you have love for one another" (John 13:35). Without question, loving relationships among believers speak volumes about the authenticity of our commitment to Jesus. But they don't communicate *how* to become a follower of Jesus. The gospel isn't transmitted by osmosis from good works to sinful hearts.

The gospel is communicated through the Word and words about the Word—verbally or by a meaningful equivalent (like sign language, Braille, printed materials, etc.). Just as nature reminds a person of God's wonder, Christian fellowship can show a person God's love. But neither communicates the death, burial, and resurrection of Jesus—why it happened or how to access its saving power. There are many positive results from being devoted to fellow believers. Spontaneously communicating the gospel solely by your sterling example isn't one of them! Jesus, who perfectly modeled Christian devotion and fellowship, still had to explain Himself and invite people to follow Him. Do you really think your life is so remarkable your example can accomplish what Jesus' life didn't? Not likely!

Being deployed, rather than dispersed, means you intentionally speak the gospel in your circle of influence. Your family and friends, your co-workers and workout buddies, your neighbors and classmates all become your missions field. Your daily life becomes an adventure of praying for, living among, and talking with people who are in the process (at some point along the way) of committing themselves to Jesus. Your role is to help as many people as possible move closer and closer to making that commitment, and to help those who are ready to submit themselves to Jesus to do so.

While this perspective is foundational, there is also another way to connect with your community and share the gospel. To do it, you will need to adopt an approach used by international missionaries—an infiltration strategy—designed to build new bridges over which the gospel can pass. Let's learn what that means as you continue your quest to become more effective talking with people about Jesus.

CHAPTER 6

INFILTRATING YOUR COMMUNITY WITH THE GOSPEL

WHILE DISCUSSING THE NEED to mobilize more believers to talk about the gospel in public settings, a Christian leader told me, "I couldn't agree more about the need to infiltrate the community with the gospel. We have an exciting example of doing this in our church." He then told this story: A young woman developed a passion for ministry to unwed mothers. She asked a few business leaders in her church to form an advisory committee (later to become a board after the ministry incorporated). She rented a house, advertised the program, and was soon caring for several women. The ministry flourished as one woman after another moved into the house, gave birth, was helped to establish a healthy parenting lifestyle, and heard about Jesus. "That," he concluded, "is a great example of infiltrating the community with the gospel."

Well, not exactly. It's a good example of a church launching a ministry to meet a pressing need. But it's *not* an example of taking the gospel to community venues. My friend's interpretation of this ministry as being "in the community" illustrates how difficult it is for many Christians to conceive of sharing the gospel outside venues controlled by a church or ministry organization. Many believers, especially those who have been Christians for a long time, have difficulty conceiving of infiltrating culture as a primary means of sharing the gospel. We have a hard time breaking out of our Christian subculture's way of thinking.

INSIDE THE BUBBLE

Prior to becoming a Christian, you probably had an extensive network of community-based relationships. For example, you played softball with your company's team, went to a ceramics class at the YMCA, or volunteered in the classroom where your children attend school. As your lifestyle changed (becoming more churchcentric), if you are like many believers, you lost connection with people from these other places. Sometimes, that's a required adjustment to help break old, destructive behavioral patterns in your life. Unfortunately, at other times, it cuts us off from people who need to hear the gospel.

Changing your lifestyle to obey biblical mandates regarding church fellowship is important. Some former activities, like carousing with immoral friends, had to stop when you submitted to Jesus as Lord. Behavior that contradicts clear instructions from the Bible must be avoided. Not doing so perpetuates a sinful lifestyle and will, ultimately, deaden your spiritual sensitivity and stunt your spiritual growth. You also may need to avoid other activities, though not inherently sinful, because they were too important in your former life. They skewed your past priorities and will prohibit future spiritual development. Any all-consuming activity can become an idol— a false god controlling your behavior and relationships.

Carney coached girls' softball, spending almost every weekend practicing or traveling with an elite team. When he became a Christian, he had stepped away from that commitment to establish a relationship with a church, focus on his spiritual development, and devote more time to his family. After a while, he resumed coaching— albeit with a more reasonable schedule—and found the relationships with players and their families fertile ground for sharing his testimony. Through those friendships, several adults and teenagers made commitments to Jesus.

MAKE AN INTENTIONAL CHOICE TO BREAK OUT OF THE CHRISTIAN SUBCULTURE.

Distancing yourself from your former community may happen inadvertently if your church creates a menu of activities to replace corresponding community programs. Churches build recreation centers to replace local gyms, sponsor sports leagues as an alternative to public leagues, and create senior citizen activities to compete with community-based programs. Churches also create ministries as "Christian versions" of community programs—children's homes instead of foster care, Christian schools instead of public schools, or benevolence ministries instead of government-sponsored homeless shelters. All these church or ministry-based activities create a Christian subculture—a way of life with limited contact with people in the world around us.

While there's nothing wrong with churches creating these ministries (they are often quite helpful), they can have the unintended consequence of isolating you from relationships with unsaved people in your community. Being "involved in the community" then becomes a euphemism for "supporting church-sponsored programs for the community." While they sound similar, they really aren't the same thing. The first is essential for sharing the gospel as life happens. The second can become a well-intentioned, but isolating substitute for being with lost people. Some Christians, including many church and ministry leaders, must make an intentional choice to break out of the Christian subculture. As my daughter once told me, "Living your life surrounded by Christians is like being in a big bubble. You've got to break out if you want to reach lost people." Breaking out of the Christian subculture means connecting people with the gospel, in their setting, by infiltrating your relational network with the good news about Jesus.

ADOPTING INFILTRATION STRATEGIES

Churches today, and most Christians who support their work, focus on *attraction* and *engagement* strategies to communicate the gospel to their community. Let's define those two concepts. An attraction strategy is a Christian event or program designed to accommodate unbelievers and introduce them to Jesus Christ. For example, seeker-friendly worship services or Christian coffeehouses are attraction strategies. They are designed for Christians to invite unbelievers to hear the gospel, experience Christian fellowship or worship, and observe Christian community.   *infiltration*

An engagement strategy is an event or program designed to extend ministry to unbelievers and introduce them to Jesus. For example, church-based sports programs or neighborhood block parties are engagement strategies. The home for unwed mothers described at the beginning of the chapter is another good example. Engagement strategies are designed to invite non-Christians to participate in activities with believers, sample Christian fellowship, and hear the gospel.

Both attraction and engagement strategies have their place and shouldn't be abandoned. They are, however, increasingly inadequate for gospel penetration of a post-Christian or never-Christian culture across North America. An *infiltration* strategy must also be promoted by churches and celebrated by church leaders.

What is an infiltration strategy and how does it differ from attraction and engagement strategies? An infiltration strategy is the deployment of believers (concept from the previous chapter) throughout the culture to introduce unbelievers to Jesus Christ in their context. It's the category of evangelism strategies that goes hand in hand with talking about Jesus as life happens. Infiltration strategies bring intentionality to the unscripted conversations of everyday relationships.

Consider the following comparisons to help clarify the differences in these three approaches. For example, starting a church-sponsored softball league for the community is an attraction strategy. Creating a church-sponsored softball team and playing in a community-sponsored league is an engagement strategy. Joining your company's softball team—practicing, playing, and staying for the aftergame refreshments—is an infiltration strategy. Inviting a friend to Sunday School is another example of an attraction strategy. Organizing a Bible study at your workplace and inviting friends is an engagement strategy. Volunteering as a corporate chaplain and sharing the gospel in the workplace is an infiltration strategy. Another attraction strategy is starting a children's home. An engagement strategy is developing a church-sponsored mentoring program for at-risk children. An infiltration strategy is becoming a foster parent through the state-controlled children's services division.

Many Christians find living an infiltration strategy lifestyle more difficult than participating in attraction or engagement strategies. There are several reasons for this, some rooted in the characteristics of infiltration strategies and others caused by churchcentric activities which aggressively support the other two strategies.

Christians aren't in control. The first reason infiltration strategies are difficult is Christians don't control the venues where they happen. These venues are definitely unscripted. Notice in the list above a common characteristic of infiltration strategies—someone other than a church board or Christian leader sets the rules, controls the schedule, establishes the policies, and most importantly, determines the values of the organization or program. This is a problem for many Christians who are intimidated by secularization, which contradicts their core values. International missionaries live like this all the time. We can learn from their example and embrace living among secular people as an opportunity to model and speak the gospel—even when we can't control the setting.

Rick works for a local coffee shop. It isn't a Christian company or ministry. No problem for Rick. He befriends fellow employees and tells them about Jesus. He has turned down job opportunities with Christian ministries so he can remain employed among unbelievers. Active in his church, he refuses to allow his entire social circle to fill with Christian friends. He goes to work not just to make money, but also to make friends with people who need to hear the gospel. He shares the gospel as life happens.

Tom is on the board of a local sports league. Most board meetings are challenging to sit through—lots of profanity, self-serving decisions, gossip, and immature posturing. It would be much more pleasant to serve on the committee that oversees his church's sports program. Yet, he stays in the community—modeling Christian integrity, making friends, and sharing the gospel. He once said, "After every meeting, I feel like I need to go home and take a shower." A Christian sometimes wades through some cultural sewage to deliver the gospel.

Too many Christians, especially leaders, can't fathom intentionally choosing to work or play outside the Christian subculture. Our seminary's primary campus is in the San Francisco Bay Area, a hotbed of politically liberal, religiously indifferent, secular thought. There aren't many churches—and fewer large churches with plentiful resources—since evangelicals comprise about 3 percent of the total population. When prospective students visit our area, they usually reach one of two conclusions: Some wonder how they can live with no Christian schools, recreation programs, day-care centers, or extensive church ministries to support their Christian faith. In short, they wonder how they will survive without a Christian subculture—a comfort zone they aren't prepared to leave. Those students don't normally choose our school.

On the other hand, some prospective students are drawn to our area because it requires joining the community to find the services listed above. They understand the absence of a Christian subculture means they must infiltrate the culture, and in doing so build relationships with unbelievers. Believers who consider themselves deployed, not just dispersed, see their role as infiltrating cultural networks and systems with the gospel. These Christians see their setting as a gold mine of spiritual opportunity. They embrace living where very few people are followers of Jesus.

Christians fear compromise. A second reason infiltration strategies are difficult is Christians are afraid of being tainted by the culture. They are uncomfortable hearing profanity, sharing meals where alcohol is served, sitting in the smoking section, hearing off-color humor, or socializing with secular people. They prefer insulation from offensive aspects of culture, rather than infiltration of it. Christians also shy away from serving on boards, committees, or organizations with people who don't share all their values.

This raises an important question related to personal holiness among deployed believers: Do you violate Christian standards by befriending people who behave in sinful ways? The answer is a resounding no! Jesus modeled living among sinful people, yet without sinning. Relating to people who make poor choices isn't the same as making those choices yourself. Christians must have the spiritual self-discipline to relate to unbelievers based on who they are (a person made in God's image), not what they do (act reprehensibly toward God). As you infiltrate culture with the gospel, you must learn to relate to people without judging them. You love people, overlooking their inappropriate behavior because you know it's a symptom—not the cause—of their lostness.

One word of caution, however, as you develop relationships with non-Christians in secular situations. Some behavior may be so tempting it would be wise for you to avoid associating with people involved in it until you are sufficiently capable of resisting the temptation. For example, if you were a compulsive gambler prior to your conversion, it would not be a good idea for you to "infiltrate the culture" at your local casino. Newer Christians often must break old patterns by completely disassociating themselves from past behavior (and sometimes friends involved in it). This may be a temporary decision during a season of spiritual development or a lifelong choice if the temptation is unrelenting. You must be mature enough in your faith to resist temptations while you reach out to unbelievers, as well as recognize situations you need to avoid all together.

It's also important to remember, some behavior is always inappropriate for Christians. For example, my outreach to men often includes going out to restaurants with them where they drink alcohol. Being with them while they drink isn't a problem for me. I'm not compromised by their behavior, nor is consuming alcohol tempting to me. But other venues would be a problem. If they suggest we go to a strip club after dinner, I decline. That environment would undermine my moral purity, compromise my integrity as a leader, and damage my marriage. Infiltrating culture by engaging unbelievers isn't a license to sin or otherwise justify inappropriate behavior. Spiritual discernment and personal discipline are required to walk these fine lines.

Christians lack confidence in their faith. A third reason some Christians find infiltration strategies difficult is poor spiritual esteem. They aren't really sure about their faith's legitimacy in the marketplace of competing religions and ideologies. They feel threatened when unbelievers share gut-honest, critical opinions of their church or Christianity in general. These believers lack a robust faith capable of standing up in the marketplace. What passes for discipleship today has too often produced weak-willed believers without the spiritual stamina to make a difference in secular settings. This type of faith is a "greenhouse faith"—only capable of thriving in controlled environments. To infiltrate culture with the gospel requires a faith able to withstand hurricane force opposition—spiritual, philosophical, and ideological.

A few years ago, my oldest son attended a football camp in the southern part of the United States. On the Sunday before the camp began, we attended a very large church in a nearby town. Several teenagers—many of them cute Southern belles—noticed my son, welcomed him to the church, and said they hoped he was moving

MY FAITH IS
EITHER REAL,
OR IT ISN'T.

to the area. There were probably more high school students in that worship service than total attendance at our church in Oregon. Over lunch, I asked him, "Son, do you regret not growing up in the South with big churches and large numbers of Christians—especially Christian girls?" He replied, "Not really. In Oregon, if you're a Christian you have to really mean it. Everyone was nice to me today, but they have a lot of support in a place like this. There are only a couple of Christians in our football program (more than 100 young men). My faith is either real, or it isn't. There's no reason to be a Christian where we live unless you really mean it. No, growing up in Oregon has been good for me. It's made my faith stronger."

How do you feel when you are the only Christian in the conference room? The only Christian on the night shift at your factory? The only believer in your bridge club? The only person in your bowling league who doesn't think "Jesus Christ" is an expletive? If you are, in one way that's good! It means you have a wide-open opportunity to model the gospel and tell the story of Jesus. If you don't see your situation in a positive light, why do you have so little confidence in your faith? Do you have spiritual doubts? Resolve them through Bible study and Scripture memory that develops the mind of Christ in you (1 Corinthians 2:16). Do you have intellectual questions? Study sound apologetic resources that address your concerns. Are you plagued by a sense of spiritual weakness? Focus on God's grace and the empowering work of the Spirit. Is lack of integrity—not living what you claim to believe—undermining your faith among your lost friends? Stop making excuses and change your behavior.

The Christian faith is personally transforming, intellectually defensible, spiritually empowering, and practically livable in every life setting. You can develop the spiritual self-esteem to represent the gospel boldly, without reticence, to the people in your circle of influence. You can have an authentic faith, confidently shared no matter the spiritual climate.

Churches seldom celebrate infiltration lifestyles. Adopting infiltration strategies is also difficult because church and denominational leaders seldom celebrate Christians who adopt this lifestyle. They celebrate what happens in church buildings (attendance, baptisms, and offerings) or what happens through church programs (including those directed toward unbelievers). Church members who devote significant time to infiltrating the community with the gospel aren't often recognized or honored.

One church countered this trend by celebrating the many families in their church who were involved in community sports programs. They formed a support group to help those families develop more intentional strategies to reach other families with the gospel. Notice they did not form a sports-based church outreach program. Church leaders encouraged families to stay involved with their secular leagues. The church organized a once-a-month meeting for prayer, sharing success stories, problem-solving difficult situations, and distributing resources for witnessing to athletes or their family members. When a person professed faith in Jesus, it was reported to the support group. If a person associated with one of the teams made a public decision to follow Jesus in a worship service, church leaders highlighted their commitment as the results of the work of their deployed, sports-participating members.

Another church committed to being the primary provider of foster care families in their county. As families were trained and deployed through the state-funded, state-controlled system, the church formed a support group to troubleshoot problems and facilitate greater success among its families involved in this effort. Notice they did not form a parallel ministry. Instead this church has become the go-to source for foster care in their county, embraced by secular leaders and making a significant impact infiltrating never-before-touched segments of their community.

Christians with a robust faith must infiltrate public schools, sports programs, chambers of commerce, factory floors, country clubs, foster care systems, and countless other venues with the gospel. Believers who choose this path must be celebrated, not criticized, by church leaders and viewed as missionaries to their communities. These believers aren't merely social workers or spiritual activists. They are gospel tellers who seek intentional ways to introduce Jesus to every person. They are more than a spiritual presence. They talk about Jesus, win converts, and make disciples. Their courage to go without a script—meeting people where they are on their terms—should be lauded and rewarded. When the results of their work become evident, wise church leaders celebrate the victories and encourage others to join the effort.

IMPLEMENTING INFILTRATION STRATEGIES

Christians must learn to think of themselves as deployed, not just dispersed throughout the culture. Christians are already embedded in schools, companies, and neighborhoods where they study, work, and live. You don't need to "get outside the walls of the church." You live there already. Every Christian has a relational network, even though some may be limited because of years of immersion in the Christian subculture. When you adopt a witnessing lifestyle, becoming more connected to your community will involve two options—maximizing current relationships and/or purposefully creating new relationships for personal evangelism. Consider these examples of both options for infiltrating your world with the gospel.

George committed his life to Jesus, but decided to keep racing automobiles as his avocation. He started telling his friends about his conversion and encouraging them to become followers of Jesus. His race team organized a car show, on a church parking lot, to connect his racing friends to his church friends. Note this distinction: George connected his lost friends to his church friends but in the context of an activity central to their lives, not those of church members. He maximized existing relationships for sharing the gospel.

Lisa, a young mother, moved to a new community and wanted to establish friendships with other women like her. She could have joined a church-based group for mothers of preschoolers. Nothing wrong with that! A nearby local church offered a Christian-focused program with unbelievers welcome—a classic engagement strategy. But Lisa wanted to meet more women who needed to know Jesus. So, she joined a local play group operated by a community center. Lisa met about a dozen women who became her friends. Over time, she discovered none of them were Christians—or had any connection to a church. Lisa had biweekly opportunities to interface with women who shared her life concerns, pressures, and frustrations. It was easy to talk about how her faith was a source of solutions to these issues. Talking about Jesus was part of the conversation—along with diaper rash, dealing with colic, developmental concerns, and laughter about the funny things children do. Choosing to infiltrate a play group is an example of initiating new relationships for the purpose of sharing the gospel. And with kids around, definitely unscripted!

Whether you are maximizing existing relationships or initiating new ones to share the gospel, here are four principles that will help you implement infiltration strategies. These simple steps will improve your effectiveness in having conversations about Jesus.

Be intentional. Sometimes, the perspective described in this chapter is derided as an excuse for diminished church involvement or a watered-down relational approach that soft sells witnessing. Both of those criticisms can be true if you aren't intentional about sharing the gospel. Being unscripted doesn't mean being unintentional. Living a good life among unbelievers and hoping your spiritual aura effects life change is insufficient. Intentional strategies make the difference. One of the simplest strategies is making a prayer list of unbelieving friends and praying regularly for their salvation. This practice accomplishes two things. First, it asks God for something within His will and with biblical precedent (see chap. 2). Second, it continually sensitizes you to the spiritual needs of the people you are praying for.

Another intentional strategy is maintaining a record of your progress in sharing the gospel with your friends. Randy kept a small notebook in his car with a page for each person he was trying to reach with the gospel. It also doubled as his prayer list (described above). Any time he had a spiritual conversation with one of this friends, he noted it. He also included significant life events (births, marriages, promotions, etc.) as well as life struggles (sicknesses, deaths in their family, etc.) that might contribute to his connecting the gospel to them. While you may be so relationally sensitive you don't need a spiritual spreadsheet, keeping records of your witnessing attempts and the progress you are making can be helpful.

A third intentional strategy is having Christian literature, DVDs, CDs, and website addresses to give to others. When witnessing to friends and family members, the gospel is often shared incrementally. My friend Braden responded very openly to a question I raised about his spiritual background. We talked for about 20 minutes about the gospel. He had to return to work, so I offered him a gospel tract about salvation. He agreed to read it. The next time we met, our conversation was based on follow-up questions from the tract.

When a friend expresses spiritual interest, one very good way to extend the dialogue is to share a resource related to their concern. Randy, the same man mentioned earlier with the notebook, also taught me this practice. He always had a ziplock bag of materials addressing various life issues from a Christian perspective in his car and office, ready to distribute at a moment's notice. Now, with electronic resources, you can text or email a web address as a follow-up to many conversations and keep records of witnessing encounters in your phone.

Be available. Engaging people with the gospel takes time. My commitment to being a corporate chaplain means declining other ministry opportunities. It also takes time away from family and personal activities. Finding the balance in all this is important, but so is making time to build and maintain witnessing relationships. Part of my responsibility is being available, having time for spontaneous conversations; answering phone calls; returning text messages and emails; sharing meals; and attending weddings, funerals, and baby dedications. Most of these events are unscripted, yet a timely response is necessary. Seizing the moment and striking while the opportunity is hot for a ministry connection is an essential part of sharing the gospel as life happens.

To create flexibility in your schedule may require you to evaluate how you are spending your time. Are you completely enmeshed in Christian activity to the exclusion of relational involvement with lost people? If so, some transactional adjustments of your schedule may be required. Transactional adjustments mean you must take something off of your schedule before you can put something else on it. You can't keep adding more and more. The formula for healthy schedule changes is "minus one precedes plus one." As you create more time for connecting with unbelievers, you must also decide what current commitments must be deleted before anything new can be added.

Another part of this is creating margin in your life so you can respond to serendipitous opportunities for conversations about Jesus. When a sportswriter stopped me at the ballpark and asked me to lunch to talk about his spiritual questions, it immediately became a priority. Other obligations had to be pushed back or canceled. Keeping your schedule flexible enough to respond to unexpected opportunity is challenging, but essential for connecting with people—on their timetable—about the gospel.

Be yourself. People can sense a phony. If you want to share the gospel, living an authentic life—not a perfect life—is essential. The people you live and work around know the real you, so be yourself. Be a genuine Christian, not a person playing the part or acting a role. One devilish lie is that Christians can't witness to people who know them well unless they live a perfectly committed life around them. Not true. Unbelievers know you aren't perfect—so stop thinking you have to be. It's better to admit your mistakes, apologize for them, and move on rather than try to hide them. Most non-Christians will respond positively, respecting your honesty and still being willing to listen when you talk about the gospel.

Trevor is trying to live out a Christian lifestyle at work. After a series of problems with his boss—some his fault, some not—he exploded in anger in front of his co-workers. He vented his frustration is blunt terms, including profanities he thought were erased from his vocabulary. Trevor called me, discouraged, feeling his witness was lost with his fellow workers. My counsel: go to work tomorrow, accept responsibility for your actions, and apologize. To his surprise, the response was positive among his co-workers who told him, "No problem, just forget it." A genuine apology, expressed humbly, defuses conflict and restores most relationships. Your non-Christian friends know you aren't perfect. Authenticity trumps duplicity every time, so admit your mistakes and move on.

Be patient. The final step to implementing an infiltration strategy is patience. Some people are ready to hear the gospel and respond now. Share the gospel, win them to faith in Jesus, and disciple them to spiritual strength. Many people, however, take time to open themselves to the gospel. You may pray for months or years, always looking for an opportunity to share the gospel, yet feel stymied in the process. When you finally introduce the gospel into the conversation, the response may be tepid or even resistant. Many witnesses give up at this point, assuming they have failed. Not necessarily.

Most people open themselves to the gospel over time. God orchestrates circumstances to bring unbelievers to the end of self-trust, convince them of His love, remove objections to faith, and clarify the gospel as a grace gift apart from any works. They process the gospel slowly, truth dawning on them over time rather than having a dramatic revelation. Some unbelievers are watching you, wanting to know if the gospel is really transformational before making their commitment. Finally, some lost people are just plain stubborn—self-sufficient and unwilling to repent. Unfortunately, being broken by life's disappointments is often part of their path back to God. Your steady friendship may facilitate their progress to salvation through the pain of a broken life.

When you commit to talking openly about Jesus, you will find people more open to the gospel than you imagine. After 30 years of sharing my faith, my overall impression is most unbelievers are either open to or at least tolerant of gospel dialogue. My truly negative witnessing experiences can be counted on one hand. Most non-Christians, when approached appropriately, aren't antagonistic about discussing religious issues—including hearing a Christian's testimony and the story of Jesus.

Many of the barriers to sharing our faith have been erected by us, not by the people around us. Religious barriers to communicating the gospel can be removed, but only by the same people who built them. You can remove religious barriers to sharing your faith and communicating the gospel. The next chapter will teach you how to do it.

CHAPTER 7

BREAKING BARRIERS TO REACHING PEOPLE WITH THE GOSPEL

W HEN JESUS SPENT TIME WITH UNBELIEVERS—
like "tax collectors and sinners"—the people most upset
by His actions were religious leaders. Matthew was a
tax collector (a group despised for collaborating with the Romans)
who became a follower of Jesus. After his conversion, he hosted a
dinner party to introduce Jesus to his friends. When they learned
Jesus ate with sinners, the Pharisees (top-level religious leaders)
were aghast and indignant. They asked Jesus' disciples, 'Why does
your teacher eat with tax collectors and sinners?' . . . Jesus said, 'It is
not the healthy who need a doctor, but the sick. . . . I have not come
to call the righteous, but sinners'" (Matthew 9:11–13 NIV).

Jesus made this clear: His life would be marked by personal,
direct contact with people the religious elite considered unworthy
and inferior. He intended to connect with real people in unscripted
life situations—as life happened.

Why were the Pharisees so upset about this? They had created an elaborate system of ritual hand-washing and personal cleansing to justify themselves before God, gain favor among their peers, and keep up appearances of holiness in their community. While the Old Testament called for careful food preparation and personal cleanliness (Leviticus 11–15), the Pharisees added to those requirements with man-made legalistic rules and regulations. Jesus, as a religious leader, was expected to toe the line and avoid eating with (and thus associating with) unclean people like Matthew's friends. On another occasion, Jesus confronted the Pharisees for their duplicity saying, "Now you Pharisees clean the outside of the cup and dish, but inside you are full of greed and evil" (Luke 11:39). Jesus' scandalous behavior (eating with unclean people) and rebuke of their legalism riled the Pharisees, fueled their jealousy, and ultimately contributed to their role in Jesus' crucifixion (Luke 11:53–54).

This pattern is repeated throughout the Gospels. The most vitriolic opposition to Jesus was from religious leaders, including His own disciples who sometimes questioned His methods and approaches (Matthew 16:21–23). Unbelievers, even those who didn't commit to Jesus, were drawn to Him and wanted to be around Him. The barriers to lost people following Jesus in the first century were largely erected by religious leaders and the religious community. It's the same in our day. Religious people often put up barriers—often inadvertently—that limit our effectiveness in sharing the gospel and discourage people from committing themselves to Jesus. What kind of barriers do we erect? The following is a top-ten list of obstacles to people hearing the gospel, all put in place by Christians. The good news is removing these barriers is also within our control. After considering each barrier, key solutions will also be proposed at the end of each section in this chapter. As you read, ask God to make you part of the solution, not a perpetuator of the problems limiting the gospel's expansion.

REDEFINING WITNESSING

One problem that limits effective evangelism is defining witnessing as living a good life and allowing your example to be your witness. It's important to live consistently, demonstrating integrity between your beliefs and actions to non-Christians. Your example is part of your testimony. Sometimes, this definition of witnessing is popularized by sayings like, "You may be the only Jesus another person ever sees" or "You may be the only Bible your friend ever reads." While those sentiments may motivate you to live out your faith, they aren't accurate statements describing an effective witnessing methodology.

No person—not even Jesus—has ever lived a life that spontaneously communicated the gospel. Jesus came as the Word (John 1), not the Example, and spoke the gospel. His ministry included explaining the gospel, preaching the gospel, and asking people to respond to the gospel—all verbal activities necessary for adequate and accurate communication. If Jesus had to verbally tell His story, despite His perfect life lived among unbelievers, how can you realistically expect to communicate the gospel effectively by simply living a godly example? It can't be done. Lifestyle evangelism isn't about living in such a way the gospel is communicated as others observe your behavior. Lifestyle evangelism is living in such a way that your verbal witness has credibility when you share it. In short, your walk with Jesus matches your talk about Jesus.

Another related redefinition of witnessing is serving others in Jesus' name as your witness. Service is a powerful expression of Christian discipleship since, "If anyone wants to be first, he must be the last of all and servant of all" (Mark 9:35). Servant evangelism projects are growing in popularity today (more about this later in this chapter). Through service, love is demonstrated, and those who favor this definition conclude unbelievers "will know that you are My disciples, if you have love for one another" (John 13:35). They may know we are Christians by the love we show them and each other. But that doesn't mean our service communicates to unbelievers how to become followers of Jesus. Service must be coupled with an explanation of the gospel to be an effective witnessing method.

One of the most effective methods of servant evangelism today is disaster relief. When volunteers show up after a hurricane, tornado, earthquake, or tsunami, the love they demonstrate earns them a ready audience. Burt, a veteran worker, told me, "When we're cleaning up a mess, we remember the people come first." Disaster-relief workers are trained to initiate conversations, listen to concerns, process grief, and share the gospel with people often made vulnerable by their recent experience. Cleaning up fallen trees, mucking out after a flood, or serving hot meals all demonstrate the love of Jesus; but those actions don't—in and of themselves—communicate the gospel. Servant evangelists set the stage for sharing the gospel by their actions; then tell the story of Jesus so hurting people can be saved.

Solution: Reject any redefinition of personal evangelism that doesn't include sharing the plan of salvation. Adopt a definition of sharing the gospel that includes communicating these essentials: God's love; humanity's sin; Jesus' death, burial, and resurrection; and every person's opportunity and obligation to respond.

TOLERANCE UNDERMINING PERSUASION

Tolerance has been redefined in this generation. The word formerly meant patience and respect for persons who held positions with which you disagree. Postmodern thought has redefined the word to mean acceptance of every viewpoint as equally valid. Tolerance now means you embrace every ism, tenet, or dogma as true. Suppose you believe Jesus is the only way of salvation but your friend believes all religions lead to heaven. Tolerance once meant you honored your friend's opinion while patiently trying to persuade him or her to change their mind. Now, tolerance means you affirm your friend's belief as equally valid or equally true with your position. This new politically correct definition of tolerance denies absolute truth and pronounces "true" whatever any person believes to be true. It's the ultimate idolatry—venerating personal opinion as absolute truth.

Christians sometimes adopt this point of view out of fear of judging others. They take seriously Jesus' warning, "Do not judge, so that you won't be judged" (Matthew 7:1). They are determined not to be judgmental, preferring to defer and avoid confronting anyone about their behavior or beliefs. Unfortunately, this understanding of avoiding being judgmental smacks more of the modern definition of tolerance than the genuine biblical ideal. Being judgmental, as defined by Jesus, is holding people to a standard you aren't willing to meet yourself or criticizing people for their lifestyle choices on nonessential matters. It's not equated with diluting core convictions of the Christian faith to keep from offending another person.

The Bible is very clear—the gospel and its implications must be shared, without compromise, even among people whose

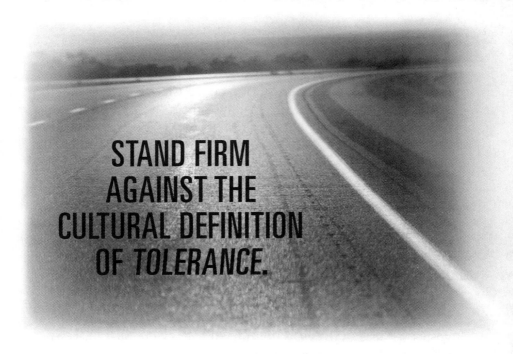

STAND FIRM
AGAINST THE
CULTURAL DEFINITION
OF TOLERANCE.

behavior and beliefs are contradicting both. A good example is Jesus' conversation with the woman at the well (John 4). She was openly immoral (John 4:18) and tried to shift the focus by starting a debate about worship (John 4:19). Jesus was nonplussed and undeterred. He kept the focus on the woman's need for a relationship with Him. Jesus didn't say, "I understand your choices. If adultery is your sexual preference and worshipping your way makes you feel close to God, then I affirm the truth as you know it." Instead, He confronted her immorality and confounded her misguided attempt to start an argument about worship practices.

Being judgmental is an attitude more than a set of words or actions. When Jesus confronted the woman at the well, something about Jesus' approach touched her deeply and positively (John 4:29). When you share the gospel, your attitude should reflect humility and gentleness. When your words are steeped in compassion, even confrontation comes across as genuine love for the other person. Your witnessing role involves persuasion, sharing the gospel, and doing all you can to convince a person to place faith in Jesus. Don't let a misguided definition of tolerance keep you from asking people to change their beliefs.

Solution: Stand firm against the cultural definition of *tolerance* as accepting all beliefs as equally true. Avoid the devilish misconception that holding to the truth of the gospel somehow judges others who disagree with you. Determine to share the gospel with compassion, persuading others in appropriate ways to follow Jesus. Remember, unscripted conversations aren't always unfocused conversations. Listen to people attentively, but talk about the gospel with boldness and clarity.

OVERCOMPLICATING SHARING THE GOSPEL

Talking about Jesus should be a simple conversation. But, like many things, we make it more difficult than it is, usually with good motives but unintended, negative consequences. In one African tribe, the word used for "American" is the same word translated "makes things too complicated." Ouch! Some witness training programs fall into this pattern. They create barriers to communicating the gospel because of their level of difficulty and subliminal message a Christian shouldn't share the gospel until they pass the "witnessing class." While personal evangelism training courses definitely have their place in church programming, we can't allow them to overcomplicate the task of sharing our faith. Take the classes your church offers! If there are no training opportunities, ask your leaders to start some. But, while being trained, avoid believing the subtle lie that witnessing is only for the experts who can master detailed curriculum.

A few Christians need in-depth, specialized training related to evangelism. There's an important role for apologists—people who make intellectually defensible arguments for the truth of the gospel. Some non-Christians with legitimate questions about Christianity will analyze and argue about religious issues. They can be quite animated in expressing their questions and concerns. Apologists are needed to take on these antagonists and convince them of the truth.

Most people who raise questions about the gospel, however, aren't motivated by intellectual opposition to Christianity. Their concerns stem from personal issues, often painful circumstances they are grappling to understand. These might include the death of a child (Why didn't God answer our prayers?), an accident that killed a friend (Why didn't God stop it from happening?), or the loss of a job (Why does God let bad things happen to me?). People asking questions like these are often looking more for compassionate reassurance of God's love than a persuasive argument about God's providence.

Another way we complicate witnessing is making it an event, rather than a normal part of the ebb and flow of life. Sharing the gospel means talking about it whenever it's appropriate in the conversation, not just on visitation night or when you make an appointment to see a friend. Witnessing is an unscripted dialogue, sometimes an ongoing dialogue with bits and parts of the gospel shared over time. Yes, there is usually a moment when you ask, "Can I take a few minutes and tell you how you can personally commit yourself to God?" But that question, and the ensuing presentation, is usually the culmination of other conversations contributing to an unbeliever's readiness to commit to Jesus. Effective witnessing is simple, direct, and a natural part of daily relationships.

Solution: Master the basics of the gospel and a simple way to present it. Learn straightforward replies to a few common questions unbelievers raise about the gospel. Focus on answering questions by unbelievers honestly, with compassion, remembering most objections to Christianity are personal or relational, not intellectual. And, if you are motivated and able, do the intellectual heavy-lifting to become an apologist for our faith.

EMBARRASSMENT ABOUT BEING A CHRISTIAN

Another barrier believers have to sharing the gospel is embarrassment about being a Christian. These feelings have several sources. One of the most frustrating is reprehensible behavior by prominent Christians. When a well-known pastor, teacher, or priest publicly confesses to sexual sin or fiscal irresponsibility, all Christians suffer a loss of credibility. The denomination or religious system of the offender may not really matter to most unbelievers. They lump us all together and broad brush the entire church with the failures of the few. It's disheartening to build relationships with unbelievers and then have them ridicule our faith when a prominent leader is revealed as a charlatan or criminal.

Sometimes, however, the problem is closer to home. When you are known as a follower of Jesus, people expect you to live up to His standards. They are often watching you, most wanting to see how faith is lived out in everyday life, a few hoping to catch you in some inconsistency they can use to justify rejection of the gospel. Because you are still a sin-tainted human, you will make mistakes, compromising your faith occasionally and failing to live out the gospel consistently. This can be embarrassing, particularly if your failures are public. Cursing a co-worker or gossiping about a neighbor contradicts your spiritual commitments and undermines your reputation as a Christian. The result can be reluctance to share your faith.

You will never live perfectly, no matter how hard you try. Christians leaders will also continue to sin, sometimes publicly embarrassing themselves and the church in general. These failures need not, however, stifle your witness. Authenticity demands frank admission of sin and apology for its negative results. The effectiveness of your witness is strengthened by honesty about your shortcomings and, when necessary, the failures of public figures. Hypocrisy is living one way while claiming another standard. It's not hypocritical to admit weakness and take responsibility for it. Doing so demonstrates the genuineness of your commitment to Jesus and your willingness to admit your mistakes. Your honesty, more than glossing over reality, will be appreciated by your unsaved friends who already know you aren't perfect.

Solution: Be honest. When your behavior is incongruent with your values, admit it and apologize. Most unbelievers will respect you more, not less, when you take responsibility for your shortcomings. Denial of your frailty, not its public display, is the death knell of your credibility as a witness. Part of living the Christian life is modeling how to confess sin, restore relationships, and serve others. Remember, denial is bad. Honesty is good.

THEOLOGICAL MURKINESS LEADING TO PRACTICAL UNIVERSALISM

The absence of doctrinal conviction among Christians is staggering. While most Christians give lip service to core beliefs related to salvation, when pressed, many waffle on the absolutes demanding conversion. The Bible plainly teaches, "For all have sinned and fall short of the glory of God" (Romans 3:23). This contradicts the common humanistic assumption people are essentially good. The Bible says, "It is appointed for people to die once—and after this, judgment" (Hebrews 9:27). This countermands the claim God kindly overlooks our rebellion against Him. Jesus claimed, "I am the way, the truth, and the life. No one comes to the Father except through Me" (John 14:6). If Jesus really meant this (and He did), then the popular idea that all religious belief, if sincerely held, assures eternal life is wrong, tragically wrong.

These are only a few examples of the clear doctrinal positions outlined in the Bible concerning salvation. Admittedly, these are hard sayings. They can't be dismissed, however, just because they are difficult to stand up for. When challenged, you must hold these positions—gently but firmly. This can be painful when you are called a narrow-minded fundamentalist, religious legalist, or intolerant bigot for upholding biblical convictions. The stakes are too high, however, to compromise these key doctrines demanding the conversion of unbelievers.

When you forsake these biblical positions, adopting instead the alternate conclusions—people are essentially good, God takes everyone to heaven, and Jesus is only a friendly teacher—you become a Universalist. While you might chafe at that conclusion and reject the formal title, theological murkiness naturally leads to practical Universalism. Jesus' uniqueness and the narrowness of the way of salvation are voided. These erroneous positions undermine sharing the gospel and calling for conversion because there's no gospel to share or salvation needed. Maintaining theological conviction isn't just important for professors at seminaries, it's essential for sustaining the urgency of your witness where you live.

Solution: If you are shaky on core Christian doctrines, do a personal study to reinforce your convictions. Read a Christian theology book written for everyday church members. Ask your pastor to organize a doctrinal study for your church or recommend a curriculum for you to lead such a class. Have the courage to uphold your convictions, not compromising them in the face of cultural pressure to embrace postmodern relativism leading to Universalism.

THEOLOGICAL CONVICTIONS THAT DEVALUE WITNESSING

Some theologians, often called Reformed or Calvinist, develop systems so dominated by the doctrine of election they eliminate the need for witnessing. The perspective of some who place themselves in these categories is God will save those He chooses apart from any human instrumentality. These extremists are a minority even among those who gladly (and in a more healthy way) wear the aforementioned labels. Any theological system that discounts the possibility of salvation for every person and the responsibility of individual Christians to share their faith is suspect and should be rejected.

The Bible affirms "for everyone who calls on the name of the Lord will be saved" (Romans 10:13). Nothing could be clearer—salvation by grace, through faith, is available to any person who receives it from Jesus (Ephesians 2:8–9). Every person in the world needs Jesus, and it's our responsibility to tell them about Him (Acts 1:8). Human instrumentality for sharing the gospel is underscored on both personal and corporate levels throughout the New Testament. Believers are portrayed with various images (see chap. 1) which carry with them personal responsibility to communicate the gospel. Corporately, preaching is mandated as a primary means for gospel transmission (Romans 10:14). When you couple these two ideas—the gospel is for everyone and humans are its means of

SHARING
THE GOSPEL IS
EVERY BELIEVER'S
PRIVILEGE.

transmission—only one conclusion can be reached: Believers must share the gospel with every person possible.

Another theological mistake undermining your responsibility for sharing your faith is making witnessing the purview of professional ministers. Some denominations make rigid distinctions between laity and clergy. Those lines of demarcation aren't so rigid in the Bible. Certainly, there were leaders with special roles in the early church and the church still needs leaders like that today. While pastors and other ministers must set the example in communicating their faith, all believers share this important work. Any theological system that divides spiritual labor into qualitative hierarchical categories should be rejected. The responsibility for personal evangelism isn't limited to a certain class of Christians. Leadership roles may be assigned to a few, but sharing the gospel is every believer's privilege.

Solution: Reject any theological convictions undermining your responsibility and opportunity to share the gospel. The gospel is for everyone. Every believer is a potential witness. No doctrinal position should be tolerated contradicting those conclusions. Don't let anyone rob you of the joy of sharing your faith and seeing people born again as a result of your witnessing.

PREOCCUPATION WITH CULTURE WARS

Another barrier to sharing your faith is anger with the culture around you. There seems so much to be angry about! The news media, entertainment companies, and educational establishment often undercut moral values Christians hold dear. We are confronted by militant groups promoting homosexuality, radical environmentalism, risks to the unborn, and unmitigated greed leading to worldwide economic uncertainty. Christians feel threatened and see the devastation these actions will leave for future generations. Some believers react with one of two extremes. Both undermine witnessing effectiveness. Some Christians retreat from the culture, immersing themselves in the Christian subculture, and avoiding contaminating contact with unbelievers. Other believers attack the culture, letting their anger drive them to condemn others who don't hold their positions—and worse, equating that with maintaining their Christian witness.

Jesus got angry on several occasions (for example, Mark 3:5 and John 11:33). In each case, His anger was directed toward His followers or the religious leaders He encountered. Jesus was never angry with unbelievers, or their collective expression as popular culture. He was confrontational with sinners, but never dismissive or overbearing with those He encountered. Paul warned against unresolved anger, "Don't let the sun go down on your anger" (Ephesians 4:26). James promised, "Man's anger does not accomplish God's righteousness" (James 1:20). If you are angry with the culture, you have chosen an ill-advised path to relate to unbelievers and effect lasting change. Engaging lost people, as personally as possible, is the best hope for cultural renewal in your circle of influence. Launching your own culture war on people around you won't change individuals or culture. It's hard to share the gospel with people who are objects of your anger.

Solution: Repent of your judgmental spirit toward lost people. Turn from anger as a strategy for cultural change. Adjust your expectations about the behavior of the unconverted. Lost people are spiritually depleted, so their poor choices shouldn't surprise you. Ask God for compassion and patience with people, particularly those who aggressively oppose your values and perspectives (and force them on your community). Confront sin, but love sinners.

SELF-FULFILLMENT AS YOUR GOAL

The self-focus of postmodern culture has infiltrated the church. Some might say it has taken over. From the health and wealth gospel promising vitality and riches for every believer to self-aggrandizing choices to spend more and more money on ourselves rather than fulfilling our gospel responsibility to the nations, the evidence seems clear. Many Christians believe the ultimate goal of the Christian life is personal fulfillment. Jesus had a different idea. He promised abundant life to His followers through the self-sacrificing decision to lose their lives for His sake. Jesus said, "If anyone wants to be My follower, he must deny himself, take up his cross, and follow Me. For whoever wants to save his life will lose it, but whoever loses his life because of Me and the gospel will save it" (Mark 8:34–35).

Too many Christians have inverted these instructions. They are determined self-fulfillment is their birthright in Christ. Their primary goals are to have their needs met, their family cared for, and their church structured to please them. They are content giving a pittance to Christian ministries, demanding church programs designed for their interests, and hiring others to do spiritual work. What's in it for me? is the most common question asked of any new proposal brought forward to change their church, class, or small group.

The church is the only organization on earth that exists for nonmembers. Christians should view the church as a fellowship on mission, not a fellowship about me. When your focus shifts from getting the gospel to others to making yourself comfortable, you will stop sharing your faith. After all, adding more people to your church will only complicate matters. Why witness? New converts are messy. Changing your lifestyle or church schedule to accommodate them detracts from your needs being met; therefore, preserving the status quo becomes the goal.

Sound too harsh? Perhaps so. Certainly Jesus meets our deepest needs and wants us to have the most fulfilling life possible. That outcome isn't in question. The method creates the tension. Jesus demands we lose our life by serving others, meeting their needs, and prioritizing their spiritual development. When we do this, we find the fulfillment we crave. When we, or our churches, serve ourselves, the fulfillment we long for remains an elusive dream.

One church planter had the courage to survey his community and ask non-Christians, "If you went to church, when would you most likely attend?" The new church scheduled its service at the most popular time for non-Christians, and the core group of Christians adjusted (hint: it wasn't Sunday morning at 11:00). This simple step communicated volumes, both to the unbelievers who felt the church really was serving them and the believers who crystallized their willingness to meet the needs of others through this decision.

Solution: The Christian life isn't a self-fulfillment program to make you healthy, wealthy, and happy. It's an opportunity to sacrifice for others, and serendipitously find meaningful life in the process. Choose to embrace change to accommodate unbelievers in your life. Remember, accommodating unbelievers isn't the same as accommodating unbelief. The former is a missional necessity, the latter an unhealthy compromise. Give yourself away meeting the needs of non-Christians at your workplace or in your neighborhood. Get the focus on others, not on your needs, and your sense of self-fulfillment will deepen exponentially. You will also find new joy in sharing the gospel as a natural outgrowth of living to serve others.

POOR DEFINITION OF CHRISTIAN COMMITMENT

Being involved in a church is vital for Christian fellowship and growth. While the focus of this book is getting you involved more intentionally with non-Christians, forsaking all church participation (even for the goal of reaching more lost people) is unwise. You must be involved in a healthy church—attending worship, participating in Bible study, giving generously, and serving in areas for which you are gifted and motivated.

While church participation is vital, it has become equated with Christian commitment and discipleship. Supporting a church program—with your presence and presents—has become the definition of discipleship. Participation has replaced transformation as the defining quality of a sanctified life. Genuine commitment to Jesus, however, is demonstrated by life transformation, not by showing up for a program. An authentic disciple's character, motives, and behavior slowly and steadily become more Christlike. That's the essence of being a disciple. Part of this growth is developing spiritual strength so you become a witness who sacrifices for others.

If you define commitment by participation in church programs or ministry activities, you will gradually become more and more encapsulated in the Christian cocoon. You may be rewarded, even held up as a model by fellow believers who share this definition of discipleship. But in doing so, you will lose the spiritual blessing of being transformed to the point you become a catalyst for the transformation of others.

Solution: Commit to balanced involvement in your church and community. Commit to maintaining Christian friendships to sustain you and friendships with non-Christians as opportunities for sharing the gospel. Resist the false guilt well-meaning believers put on you for not supporting their program or project. Measure your spiritual vitality by personal transformation, not program participation.

UNDERESTIMATING THE POWER OF SERVICE

Jesus valued serving others as a precursor for calling them to commitment. He said, "The greatest among you will be your servant" (Matthew 23:11). Christians who share their faith are often frustrated by the slowness of unbelievers to open themselves to the gospel or their unwillingness to listen to a gospel presentation. One key to gaining the opportunity to share the gospel is service—meeting the needs of others on their terms.

Serving others by meeting their practical needs can be as simple as taking food to a bereaved family or mowing a lawn when a neighbor is ill. You serve a co-worker when you stay late, off the clock, and help him finish a project. You serve a single mother by offering free child care from time to time. Simple acts of kindness go a long way in communicating your genuine concern for others.

Dan's mother died. John went to the funeral. When Dan saw his friend, he blurted out, "What are you doing here?" John replied, "I thought you might need a friend today," and tears coursed down Dan's face. Many believers enjoy such supportive Christian fellowship, they forget how isolated other people live, often enduring painful events alone. Simple acts of kindness often open a person to the gospel. Other times, it takes much longer.

One pastor served a mother and her children for 25 years before she committed her life to Jesus. When she finally decided to consider the gospel, she turned to the pastor who had steadily cared for her family for all those years. He led her to faith in Jesus because of the credibility established by his consistent concern.

Solution: Embrace service as your primary method of enhancing credibility for sharing the gospel. Look for ways to show the love of Jesus to people you are trying to reach. Keep it simple. Meet real needs without expecting anything in return. Don't overlook common problems or assume someone else will take care of the situation. As you care for others, be prepared to speak about Jesus as the reason for your compassionate concern.

These ten common barriers, often put up by believers, can keep you from sharing the gospel. Take them down! Make sure you remove any hindrance to the gospel flowing through you to the people in your circle of influence. Remember, Jesus' strongest rebukes were for religious people who put unnecessary obstacles in the path of people becoming His followers. Don't fall in with that crowd. Make sure you are creating relational pathways for the gospel to flow, not erecting barriers discouraging people from responding. Do all you can to be a conduit, not a constriction for the progress of the gospel.

CHAPTER 8

EMBRACING CHANGE
FOR THE SAKE
OF THE GOSPEL

ONE OF MY FAVORITES BUMPER STICKERS is "Change is good. You go first." Those six words capture how most people feel about change—it's fine for the other guy! An evangelistic Christian, in contrast to set-in-their-ways believers, is open to change, to being the "other guy." Sharing the gospel effectively requires adjusting your lifestyle continually, being willing to do new things in new ways to reach new people. This is a major attitude adjustment for many believers.

One youth leader taught his teenagers this response to whatever circumstances they encountered on a missions trip: "That's just the way we like it." That simple response shaped their attitude and helped them learn the flexibility needed for success in a different culture. It's a good reminder to be flexible, adjusting to changing circumstances rather than complaining about unexpected events. It's a good theme for believers who share the gospel as life happens—even when they aren't on a missions trip to another culture.

Why do Christians resist change? Why is it so hard to adopt new approaches to evangelism or accommodate the needs of new believers? Why do Christians become so entrenched in particular methods? Why is change so hard—even change needed to help us reach more people with the gospel? The answers are far too complex for a few paragraphs, but here is a summary of some key points.

First, people resist change because of a propensity toward self-preservation. Risk threatens our sense of well-being, often a false sense of safety based more on perception than reality. This leads to the second reason people resist change. Encountering change is more an emotional experience than a reasoned process. No matter the facts, some people just can't overcome their emotional roadblocks to change.

When one church decided to relocate, the decision was based on the need to create additional space for more people to have the opportunity to worship. There was no disputing the need—standing room only in multiple services every week. In theory, the church's members wanted more people to be saved and become an active part of their fellowship. When relocation was proposed, however, the response of some was negative, and emotional. One man said, "All my children were baptized and married in this church. Why are you taking my church away from me?" When the pastor replied, "We're trying to create a place for other families, in the future, to have the same privilege your family had in the past," the fellow was not satisfied. He continued to oppose the relocation, though never disputing the former facility was inadequate, but mostly focused on his sense of loss and displacement caused by having "his church taken from him."

This leads to the third reason people resist change. Potential change is often perceived as loss producing a grieflike response. When someone dies, affected people usually go through a grief process including shock, anger, denial, bargaining, and (hopefully) acceptance or adjustment. Change often carries with it a similar sense of loss. When churches change, familiar programs, methods, approaches, locations, or people are lost or replaced. Depending on the emotional attachment to former structures or relationships, this sense of loss can be profound, like grief associated with death. Intense anger, often associated with a response to death, is also a common response to significant change.

One group of churches had sponsored a children's camp for several decades. Attendance had declined to around 20 children as most of the churches dropped out of the program. The longtime leaders were determined to hang on to their methods, remembering years before when hundreds had attended and dozens of children had been converted each year. They couldn't give up their emotional attachment to past success. While their camp continued to decline, another one was created with a fresh format appealing to children today. The second camp was a strong success, reaching many children with the gospel. Some Christians cling to outdated methods or programs because of their meaningful memories of past successes, limiting their evangelistic effectiveness in the future.

Finally, a fourth reason change is difficult is because resistance is tied to the level of change required. For example, changing from pews to chairs in your worship center may not be difficult for you. After all, it's just furniture. But if your grandfather built the pews, the level of emotional investment increases exponentially, and so will your resistance to the change. Superficial changes are more easily managed. Changes affecting core values or close relationships are much more difficult. Making the personal changes necessary to adopt a more evangelistic lifestyle certainly fits this category. These are personal changes that may be quite difficult to assimilate.

Adopting a new lifestyle means you embrace change, as painful as it might be. You recognize the reasons change is difficult and overcome them. You endorse variety in methodologies for reaching people and value diversity among people. Both of these choices are contrary to the perspective many believers have today. Many Christians are settled in their methodological ways and comfortable in their monocultural community. As you focus more on personal evangelism, you will embrace the changes required for sharing the gospel and managing the response from people around you. Learning to do that is challenging, but essential. The process starts by adopting a more biblical perspective on change.

JESUS: ENCOUNTERING PEOPLE GRAPPLING WITH CHANGE

Jesus was a change agent. He changed everything from the means of atonement to establishing a new ethic for personal relationships.

It's difficult to summarize all the changes He introduced and the perspective on change He taught. A series of events in Matthew's Gospel, however, coupled with Jesus' specific teaching about change provides a good framework for understanding His core insights about this important subject.

Jesus met Matthew at his tax collection booth and asked him to become His disciple. Their dialogue was brief, but not necessarily as abrupt as it might appear. It's best understood in the context of their previous encounters, building toward the defining moment when Jesus said, "Follow Me!' And he [Matthew] got up and followed Him" (Matthew 9:9 NASB). This simple exchange reveals the most fundamental change strategy for believers. When Jesus speaks, we obey. It's that simple. Jesus demands obedience, no matter our past practices or assumptions about the future. When He directs, we respond affirmatively. We do what He says, in contrast to what we want and healthy change results. It's a natural, simple, spiritual process. The challenges, however, are twofold. First, we must discern when Jesus is speaking. We will return to that later in the chapter. Second, we must obey—a difficult, but essential choice we make.

Soon after Matthew abandoned tax collection, he hosted a dinner party for Jesus to meet his friends. As previously noted, the Pharisees were upset because Jesus ate with tax collectors and sinners (Matthew 9:11). We have already considered their concern in a different setting, their judgmental attitude creating roadblocks to people following Jesus. Now let's consider their actions in the context of learning about change. What was the Pharisees' problem? They were upset too much was changing too fast. This is one broad category of why people oppose change. They are frustrated when too many things change too rapidly. This spawns fear, uncertainty, and a sense of losing control. When people feel these emotions, they often fight back by resisting change and hardening their commitments to the status quo. It was tragically true of the Pharisees and still happens among believers today.

On the heels of his confrontation with the Pharisees, some of John the Baptist's disciples asked Jesus an interesting question. They wondered, "Why do we and the Pharisees fast, but Your disciples do not fast?" (Matthew 9:14 NASB). Jesus answered with an analogy about a bridegroom. When the groom is present, it's time to

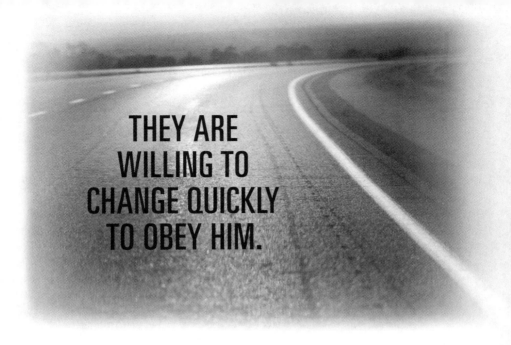

THEY ARE WILLING TO CHANGE QUICKLY TO OBEY HIM.

celebrate, not fast. Fasting is appropriate at another time. The core of their question, as it relates to the subject of change, was their frustration with Jesus not demanding more of His disciples. In essence, John's disciples were saying, "We are so committed we are even fasting. Why don't you require more from Your followers so they will be as committed as we are?" The frustration they felt was not enough was changing fast enough. This was the opposite of the Pharisees' dilemma and is also a common theme among believers today. Some Christians are innovators or early adopters. They want immediate, rapid change and are frustrated with the slow pace set by their leaders and fellow believers.

These three encounters, just before Jesus taught two key principles about change, illustrate three ways people respond to change. Some people (like Matthew) hear from Jesus and follow Him. They are tuned spiritually to Jesus' voice, willing to change quickly to obey Him, and trust the consequences of their decisions to His care. Other people (like the Pharisees) are frustrated because too much is changing too fast. They resist change, trying to lessen their threat level and slow the inevitable. Finally, some people (like John's disciples) are disappointed because not enough is changing fast enough. They are impatient with others, or with themselves, and often express those frustrations in divisive ways.

Your best response to needed change is following Matthew's example. Resist the temptation to career between the other two extremes—frustration with the pace of change, too slow or fast. Hear from Jesus and follow Him. Trust His pace, not too fast and not too slow. Believe the changes He initiates, no matter how disconcerting in the short run, will result in long-term benefit. The challenge is learning to discern Jesus' direction among the competing voices giving us input, direction, and counsel. How do you discern Jesus' direction, particularly about changing to a more evangelistic lifestyle?

First, Jesus speaks according to His purpose. His purpose, stated succinctly, was (and is) "to seek and to save the lost" (Luke 19:10). When considering lifestyle options always ask, "Will this decision likely result in more people coming to know Jesus?" If the answer is yes, there is a good probability Jesus is speaking.

Second, Jesus speaks according to His commission. His commission for you is "repentance for forgiveness of sins would be proclaimed in His name to all the nations, beginning at Jerusalem. You are witness of these things" (Luke 24:47–48). When considering a course of action, consider if it fulfills or detracts from the Great Commission (Matthew 28:18–20). If it leads to its fulfillment, there's a good probability Jesus is speaking.

Third, Jesus speaks in the context of prayer. Throughout Acts, the church sought Jesus' direction for advancing the gospel (for example, Acts 1, 6, 15). In each case, during a prayer meeting, the church discerned Jesus' direction. And, in each case, their obedient action based on their impressions produced fulfillment of Jesus' purpose and commission. If you are not praying regularly, you are not likely to discern Jesus' direction. Spiritual direction comes most clearly to prayerful believers.

Finally, Jesus speaks through church leaders. Throughout Acts, the church discerned Jesus' direction by considering His purpose and commission in an atmosphere of prayer. During or after those prayer meetings, church leaders would announce their sense of Jesus' direction to expand the gospel's reach. In each case, the church affirmed their leaders and acted on those instructions. Leaders are responsible to hear from Jesus and communicate their impressions about how to share the gospel more effectively with more and more people. Christians are responsible to follow their leaders, endorsing their spiritual directions (unless there is compelling evidence a decision is unbiblical)—particularly about evangelizing the lost.

These steps will help you discern Jesus' leadership and changes He wants you to make to enhance your effectiveness at sharing the gospel as life happens. Make decisions based on Jesus' purpose and commission, in the context of prayer, and with the concurrence of your spiritual leaders (acting within scriptural guidelines). While there is no foolproof system for making sure every change you consider originates with Jesus, you can become more discerning of His direction by using these qualifiers to analyze your options.

JESUS: TEACHING PRINCIPLES ABOUT CHANGE

In response to the question by John's disciples, Jesus taught two very important principles about change. He used common household illustrations—clothing and wineskins—to make His points. These are Jesus' most succinct statements on change and establish a framework for understanding the change process for Christians.

The first principle Jesus taught was this: real change requires real change. Jesus said, "No one patches an old garment with unshrunk cloth, because the patch pulls away from the garment and makes the tear worse" (Matthew 9:16). To paraphrase, sometimes a patch won't do. In the first century, when a garment was washed repeatedly, it shrank. When it inevitably tore, if a patch of new cloth was sewed to it and it was later washed, the patch would shrink differently from the original garment. This could result in a new tear worse than the first one. Experienced homemakers, hearing Jesus use this illustration, would have nodded with understanding. Sometimes, a patch won't work. A new garment must be made. Real change requires real change.

Most people don't mind adjustments or additions to their lives. Gradual modifications are manageable without much disruption. What troubles them is when major change, real change, is required. But some changes can't be made incrementally. Suppose, for example, the United States decided to change the driving laws so we all drove on the left side of the road. Would you want that decision phased in slowly, everyone adjusting when and if they saw fit? Or suppose you became engaged and your fiancé said, "Now I plan to start phasing out dating other people." Would that be acceptable? Not likely! Some changes are transactional, dramatic, and definitive. Old ways must be discarded. New approaches must be started. Life can't always be patched together, making incremental adjustments to moderate transitions. Sometimes, real change means real change. You must stop doing one thing and begin another.

When you decide to spend more time building relationships with unbelievers, you must simultaneously decide to stop using that time on other activities. When you decide to launch a new out-reach effort, you are simultaneously deciding not to use that time on other ministries. If you are serious about making lifestyle changes to share your faith more effectively, you will need to make transactional decisions about the use of your time. You will change your life patterns—stopping some things, starting others. Real change requires real change. Simple adjustments or additions won't produce the results you desire.

The second principle Jesus taught was this: Real change requires new structures to succeed. The word *structures* might be misleading.

REAL CHANGE REQUIRES REAL CHANGE.

Basically, this principle means intended change must be reinforced with appropriate corresponding support to sustain the effort. Jesus used wineskins as an illustration to teach this principle. He said, "No one puts new wine into old wineskins. Otherwise the skins burst, the wine spills out, and the skins are ruined. But they put new wine into fresh wineskins, and both are preserved" (Matthew 9:17). Like the cloth illustration, the wineskins illustration would have resonated with first-century hearers but needs some explanation to be understood today.

In the first century, wine was fermented and stored in wineskins (pouches made from animal hides). The fermentation process caused the wine to expand, requiring a flexible wineskin to hold the enlarging contents. An old, brittle wineskin could not adjust to those changes. Thus, new wine was put in a new wineskin—a flexible, pliable, adaptable container for the fermenting beverage. New wine required new wineskins. Placed in an old wineskin, the change process would split the container and everything would be lost.

The wineskins illustrate that making change requires new life structures, patterns, or habits to support the change. You may intend to improve in personal evangelism. But if you don't take concrete steps to reinforce your decision, to add supporting structure to your efforts, little life change will likely result. For example, if you decide to pray more for friends and family members to be saved, the change will more likely result if you create a prayer list or prayer strategy to support your decision. If you commit to share the gospel with your co-workers, you are more likely to do it if you keep a supply of gospel literature handy to distribute as needed. If you decide to spend more money on evangelism projects, you will more likely do it if you develop a personal budget or establish a saving plan to support your decision.

Jesus taught two key principles about change. Real change requires real change. Real change requires intentional, supportive structures to make it a reality. Christians who want to become more effective evangelists must implement both principles. First, decide to make substantive lifestyle changes. Second, stabilize those changes by adding the structural support necessary to make the changes last.

As you become more aware of the changes required to reach people with the gospel, if you are like many believers, you will be faced with challenges to change in two primary areas—

methodological variety and cultural diversity. Adapting in both areas is essential to continued effectiveness in reaching people with the gospel. Both require disciplined effort and spiritual determination for most believers.

EMBRACING VARIETY IN METHODOLOGY

You have a preferred way of doing most things. You drive to work the same way every day, have a favorite color predominant in your home décor, and like a certain topping on your ice cream. You probably import this propensity for comfortable repetition into ministry activities and church functions. You like to sing favorite songs, follow a familiar order of worship, hear Scripture read from a particular translation, and respond to a preferred style of preaching. This is not necessarily bad. There's nothing wrong with enjoying spiritual comfort food.

A serious problem arises, however, when we confuse the way we prefer ministry to be done with the only way it can be done. We regiment our preferences and turn them into absolutes others must accept to have a meaningful relationship with God. For example, some Christians insist their preferred English translation is the only legitimate Bible. This is problematic on several points, not the least of which is more Christians in the world worship in other languages than English. Other believers insist a certain style of music or order of service is essential for genuine worship. This is also problematic given the wide variety of ways Christians worship around the world.

There are also believers who insist on narrowly defining which evangelism approaches are legitimate. Some claim door-to-door visitation is best. Others advocate for servant evangelism. Still others insist revival meetings are required while others toss out all organized efforts in favor of organic approaches. Extroverts may enjoy street preaching. Practical servants meet needs to gain access for the gospel. Teachers think classes to educate people toward the faith are the best approach. The problem isn't having favorite methods. It's concluding your preferred methodology is the only legitimate way God uses to reach new people with the gospel. When you do that, your preferences solidify into convictions and your future flexibility is limited. Unfortunately, so is your evangelistic effectiveness.

While many good methods have been devised to communicate the gospel, the best methods have not yet been discovered. Why is this true? The world is ever-changing and ways to communicate are ever-evolving. God is a creative Father who designed a continually changing world. The seasons, the weather, and the life cycle of both plants and animals are good examples. Jesus modeled innovation by doing things people had never seen any religious leader do. He also used an unusual teaching moment to impress His disciples about the importance of remaining open to new assignments and methods.

Jesus taught a large crowd near a lake, speaking to them from one of Simon Peter's boats: "When He had finished speaking, He said to Simon, 'Put out into deep water and let down your nets for a catch'" (Luke 5:4). This is an interesting instruction given both its source and recipients. Peter was a commercial fisherman with business partners and multiple boats (Luke 5:2), yet a carpenter's son was telling an experienced fisherman how to do his job. By all rights, Peter should have rejected an amateur's advice. Instead Peter replied: "Master . . . we've worked hard all night long and caught nothing! But at Your word, I'll let down the nets" (Luke 5:5). As a result, "they caught a great number of fish, and their nets began to tear. So they signaled to their partners in the other boat to come and help them; they came and filled both boats so full that they began to sink" (Luke 5:6–7).

Peter and his partners "were amazed at the catch of fish" (Luke 5:9), causing Peter to implore Jesus to disown him. He pleaded, "Go away from me, because I am a sinful man, Lord!" (Luke 5:8). Jesus had a different outcome in mind. He used the incident to challenge Peter, call him to leave fishing, and become a kingdom leader. Jesus told Peter, "From now on you will be catching people!" (Luke 5:10).

This exchange taught Peter two important lessons about his future leadership role. First, he would be instrumental in reaching people (large numbers of people, Acts 2:41). Second, he would reach them in surprising ways. Jesus told the fishermen to lower their nets in a place they had not previously fished and at a depth they had not previously tried. They were still fishing, just doing it in new ways. Teaching Peter this principle, in the context of fishing, obviously had broader application as he progressed in his leadership role through Acts. Peter was part of many innovative moments in the early church—Pentecost (Acts 2), early inclusion of the Gentiles in the kingdom (Acts 10), and the final decision to accept Gentile converts as full-fledged Christians (Acts 15) are some examples. While he would be a "fisher of men" in one way while Jesus was alive, he would also learn to do so in ever-changing ways to accommodate the continual progress of the gospel in the early years of the church. Christians must apply the same principle today—reaching people with the best current methods while remaining open to new approaches as life situations evolve.

There are many effective ways to reach people with the gospel. No church or ministry has cornered the market on the right way to evangelize. While the focus of this book is on sharing the gospel as life happens—largely in unscripted opportunities—programmatic efforts are also productive. Personal evangelism is a solid foundation undergirding all kinds of different methods. Effective approaches to evangelism can be found in all of the following general categories of evangelistic methodology.

Direct Evangelism. This method includes door-to-door visitation, census taking in public venues, and other one-on-one encounters designed to introduce the gospel to people personally. While these approaches are sometimes intimidating (who really enjoys knocking on a stranger's door?), they are still fruitful ways to connect with people in many communities. Even when one of the methods in the following sections is used, almost every evangelistic approach ultimately comes down to one person talking to another person about Jesus. Personal, direct, one-on-one approaches are essential methods for communicating the gospel.

Ministry Evangelism. This method is also sometimes called servant evangelism. This approach includes acts of kindness like cleaning up a neighborhood, painting a school, or providing labor to refurbish homes owned by senior citizens. It can also include events like free car washes or food delivered to the homeless. Ministry or servant evangelism begins by meeting a practical need, which creates the opportunity to share the gospel. These projects often create community openness and, when done properly, lead to meaningful dialogue about the gospel.

Target Group Evangelism. This method selects a specific group of people with identifiable needs and creates strategies to deliver the gospel, often requiring an extended effort over time. Outreach to a local prison might illustrate this approach. Various kinds of ministry activities, classes, courses, counseling sessions, and recreational activities might be included in creating a climate for sharing the gospel. A target group approach assumes a fixed community of people—like men in a barracks, women in a shelter, or apartment complex residents—where relationships can be developed leading to gospel presentations.

Education Evangelism. This method uses classes or courses to communicate the gospel. Sometimes, these are directly about the gospel, like a course one church offered called Discover the Bible. It was designed for curious unbelievers who were willing to attend weekly classes for four weeks to get acquainted with the Bible and its core message—the gospel. Vacation Bible School, one of the most effective evangelism tools ever created, is another example of teaching the gospel as an evangelism strategy. Another example of this approach is need-based courses like parenting classes or marriage retreats. These venues start with an application of the Christian worldview, and then help participants discover the gospel as the foundation for the kind of life improvements they hope to make.

Event Evangelism. This method uses events ranging from evangelistic meetings in large stadiums to Super Bowl parties to communicate the gospel. Sometimes called mass evangelism, the goal of this approach is assembling a large audience and allowing a speaker (often a well-known believer appreciated by those who attend the event) to share the gospel with everyone at once.

Which method is best? Within each category, which is the best way to do each approach? Wrong questions! The better question is, which method will Jesus lead me to implement in this unique time and place to reach people with the gospel in the most effective way possible? There's an infinite variety of effective, appropriate, useful methods to communicate the gospel. Find what works in your community and do it. When the effectiveness of that method wanes, have the courage to change. Past success is often the enemy of future progress. Don't choose one method and expect it to be effective forever. Modify your approach, sharpening it as you learn more and more about the community you are trying to reach. Have the courage, when people are not responding, to do something else. Learn to fail faster, moving on without too much emotional turmoil when your preferred method is no longer effective.

VALUING DIVERSITY IN COMMUNITY

One of the most controversial and misunderstood missiological principles is called the homogenous principle. This principle correctly observes people come to faith in Jesus most readily in their community context, being asked to cross the fewest barriers possible to receive the gospel. The application of this principle is the reason international missionaries master new languages, adopt native dress codes, adjust to new time schedules, and learn to enjoy different foods. Missionaries join the community they are trying to reach, in every way possible while maintaining the integrity of the Christian ethic. When it comes to communicating the gospel, the requirement for flexibility in approach is the responsibility of the witness, not the recipient of the witness.

This is hard for many Christians. They want people to be like them, to share their values, lifestyle choices, and worship preferences—even prior to conversion! Their attitude is, "Become like me, and then you can know Jesus." While most believers would be disappointed if a missionary had this attitude, they are not so quick to recognize it or correct it when they hold it.

One church decided to reach Koreans in their area. They invited a Korean pastor to start a church in their facility. They envisioned sharing a facility, with occasional joint worship services and ministry projects (of course, structured to suit the Anglo church). An important part of a Korean church's gatherings is eating together. When the Koreans prepared their meals, the aromas were not familiar (or pleasing) to the Anglo church. The Anglos complained and said, "They can eat here, but not that awful smelling food." A consultant who had originally helped them develop a vision for planting the church asked, "But what if Jesus likes Korean food? Would you allow it to be served if He came for lunch?" They soon asked the Koreans to relocate to another facility.

It's easy to become myopic, focusing on our preferences and assuming they are the right perspective on everything from dress codes to worship styles. When we encounter other cultures, it's easy to label our way right and their way wrong. Mature believers recognize the beauty of the variety of cultural expressions among the peoples of the world. This same perspective is also required within one's own racial and linguistic community. For example, generational differences among people of similar ethnicity who speak the same language may be quite profound. Issues such as musical tastes, clothing choices, fascination with technology, hairstyles, and the preponderance of tattoos can be divisive between generations. Christians must overlook cultural differences and not allow them to limit their commitment to get the gospel to every person.

The homogenous principle is valid when it helps us design evangelistic strategies. It's important to present the gospel in the most culturally palatable way possible. You must speak the language of the culture you are addressing, literally and figuratively. When reaching Brazilians, it is important to speak Portuguese. When reaching techies or bikers, it's important to speak their "language" as well. You need to vary your approach based on the needs, perspectives, and preferences of the person you are trying to reach. Effective evangelistic Christians echo Paul's testimony, "I have become all things to all people, so that I may by all means save some" (1 Corinthians 9:22).

Valuing diversity in community is essential for effective evangelism. We are attempting to help people become Christians, followers of Jesus. We aren't trying to make them Americans, Republicans, Democrats, Conservatives, Liberals, Baptists, Methodists, Calvinists, or Pentecostals. While we may think our choices related to nationality, political party, denominational label, or theological position are best, they aren't the ultimate goal of Christian witness. Our message is the gospel—nothing more or less. Be careful you don't define the gospel in your terms and create unnecessary barriers to its communication to and acceptance by people you are trying to reach.

Change is hard! Effectively presenting the gospel requires you to be open to new ideas and approaches. Staying in your spiritual comfort zone while people perish without hearing the gospel isn't an option. Embracing variety in methodology and valuing diversity in community will help keep you pliable—and humble.

God enjoys innovation and productive change. He created a world with thousands of flowers that bloom in infinite patterns of color, shape, and form. He continually enables people to creatively discover cures for diseases, boundless sources of energy, and moving compositions of new musical sounds. God creates, and we are expected to follow His lead. Ask God for creativity to discover the most effective evangelism methods to reach your family and friends as well as the people in your community. Ask Him for courage to change, even when it's painful to implement those new ideas. Take the risk and trust God to sustain you.

CHAPTER 9

SACRIFICING FOR THE SAKE OF THE GOSPEL

I N A WORLD PROMOTING self-fulfillment as a consummate value, sacrificing for any reason is countercultural and even considered unreasonable by some. In past generations, self-sacrifice for public service, or in helping professions such as teaching or nursing, was an honored cultural value. Not so much anymore. Ministers and missionaries have also traditionally been examples of self-giving service. While many still model this value, even some Christian leaders have stopped living sacrificially and no longer challenge followers toward that ideal. In contrast, they have adopted an entitlement perspective for themselves and teach that God wants His followers to be rich, healthy, and happy. The only people, however, who enjoy these benefits are the unscrupulous preachers who teach these false doctrines and offer themselves as deserving recipients of their followers' time and money.

While some devalue sacrifice, many Christians still personify this ideal as an essential part of Christian service. Sharing the gospel will require sacrifices on your part. It will cost your two most important commodities—time and money. It may also cost you relational closeness with people you love or the privilege of exercising your rights. Sacrificing so others can hear the gospel is a self-limiting choice to put the needs of others before your own.

Before defining and describing these choices more fully, a more basic question is, does advancing the gospel really require sacrifice? Unequivocally, yes. The certainty of this answer is revealed in the example and demands of Jesus. The timeless nature of this principle means it stretches across all cultures and all generations. Sacrifice is required to send the gospel across the street or around the world, among every people and in every era—even to the people you experience as life happens.

JESUS MODELED SACRIFICE

One of the most moving descriptions of Jesus' incarnation, His taking on flesh and living among people is Philippians 2:5–8. Paul wrote:

> *Make your attitude that of Christ Jesus, who, existing in the form of God, did not consider equality with God as something to be used for His own advantage. Instead He emptied Himself by assuming the form of a slave. . . . And when He had come as a man in His external form, He humbled Himself by becoming obedient to the point of death—even to death on a cross.*

Jesus modeled self-emptying sacrifice by coming to earth and making our salvation possible.

Jesus, as part of the Godhead, has always eternally coexisted with the Father and the Spirit. He was and is fully God. When faced with the need for a Redeemer and His role in the redemptive drama, Jesus "did not consider equality with God as something to be used for His own advantage" (Philippians 2:6). Another translation of this verse is "did not regard equality with God a thing to be grasped" (NASB). Jesus gave up transcendent existence, sacrificing His state and status to identify with humankind through His incarnation. In doing so, He "emptied Himself " (Philippians 2:7). Scholars have written volumes trying to describe everything implied by those two words, yet it's still impossible to grasp their full meaning. Jesus "emptied Himself," sacrificing His position, forsaking everything pertaining to the privilege of His status as God's Son eternally reigning in the cosmos. Beyond that, He came to earth "as a man," and not just a man, but "assuming the form of a slave" (Philippians 2:7). From His birth to His death, Jesus fully identified with the gamut of human experience and condition, except for sharing our sin nature. Jesus went through the ultimate humiliation for the eternal, being subjected to death—the death of a common criminal. His execution was a crucifixion, usually reserved for criminals from the dregs of society, further underscoring His self-abasement and identification with all humanity.

Jesus modeled sacrifice. He gave up privilege and position for the good of others. He set aside His status and most meaningful relationships to meet humankind's greatest need—redemption. Jesus abased Himself—first by going through the birth process, finally by experiencing a brutal, undeserved death. In every way, Jesus sacrificed for others and established by His example the experiential authority to demand His followers do the same.

JESUS DEMANDED SACRIFICE

While there are many examples of Jesus asking His followers to sacrifice for Him or His kingdom, one of the most profound is the conclusion of a story considered in the last chapter. When Jesus impressed Peter and his partners with the miraculous catch of fish, He used the incident to call them to be fishers of men—a euphemism for helping people become Jesus' disciples. As we have already discovered, Peter was moved by the experience. He appealed to Jesus to leave him, overwhelmed by his unworthiness to be in Jesus' presence. When Jesus refused, and instead called him to give his life sharing the gospel with people, the response of Peter and his partners was immediate and dramatic: "Then they brought the boats to land, left everything, and followed Him" (Luke 5:11).

The phrase "left everything" is a stunning example of sacrifice for kingdom purposes. When those fishermen abandoned their boats that day, they "left everything." What was included in their sacrifice? First, they left their means of livelihood. They were commercial fishermen, with multiple partners sharing multiple boats. Their means of providing for themselves and their families was abandoned. Second, they left behind their status and identity in the community. As fishermen, in a time prior to refrigeration, providing fresh fish as a food source was an important role. They swapped being respected businessmen for new roles as itinerant preachers with a controversial message. Losing their identity was part of their sacrifice. Finally, they gave up their future security when they abandoned their boats. In the first century, there were no retirement plans or Social Security benefits. A person's provision as they got older was simple. They built a farm or business, turned it over to their children, and hoped they would care for them as they aged. It was more than boats left on that lakeshore. Current provision, status in the community, and future security were all abandoned for the sake of the gospel.

Jesus demands the same kind of sacrifices from His followers today. He asks us to forsake pursuing worldly gain and trust Him for "our daily bread" (Matthew 6:11). Jesus calls us to work for eternal rewards, not build a temporal kingdom that won't last (Matthew 6:19–21). He asks us to give up our identity and adopt a new identity defined by our relationship with Him (Matthew 12:46–50). We even adopt a new name—Christian—to define our core identity as Jesus' disciples (Acts 11:26). While you may not give up all these things as dramatically as those fishermen who walked away from their boats, your sacrifices over a lifetime may be just as profound. But even today, God still calls some people to make choices similar to those made by Peter and his partners.

Gordon was a successful businessman with the external trappings common to his achievements—beautiful home, vacations, cars, and so on. As a Christian, he served his church and gave generously over the years. But as he and his wife reached midlife, a desire for greater service (and sacrifice) welled up within them. After careful consideration, they decided to liquidate their company, sell their home, dispose of most of their personal property, and give their remaining years to international mission service. While some questioned the wisdom of those decisions, their children and closest friends affirmed their sacrifice and helped them with the process. Today, they are happily serving in Asia, having sacrificed much but enjoying the corresponding blessings inherent with obeying God. Like this couple, God still calls some to "leave everything" and follow Him.

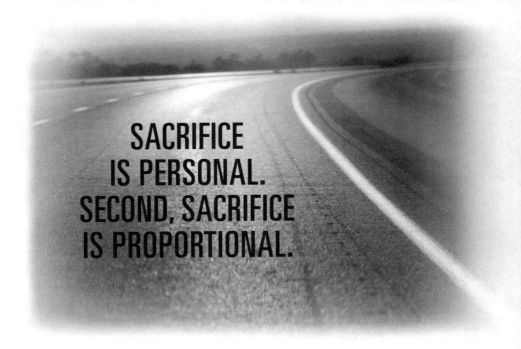

SACRIFICE IS PERSONAL. SECOND, SACRIFICE IS PROPORTIONAL.

This example raises questions about the nature of sacrifice. What defines a sacrifice? Is it the same for every person? How do you know what God wants you to give up for the sake of the gospel? Are there different expectations for different people or for various seasons of life? Let's turn our attention to defining and describing sacrifice before considering how we might obey God in this way.

UNDERSTANDING THE CONCEPT OF SACRIFICE

A sacrifice, by definition, means giving up something of value to benefit others. For many people, sacrifice is defined by and limited to giving away money or other possessions. That's one valid application. But sacrifice can also involve giving up something else of value—like time, relationships, or rights. Sacrifice, in its purest form, is setting aside your desires for the interests of others. It's self-subjugation for the benefit of another person or group of people. While these definitions of sacrifice are helpful, they don't necessarily answer the question of what constitutes a sacrificial act. There are two important components to answering that difficult question. First, sacrifice is personal. Second, sacrifice is proportional. Sorting out and applying those two principles will help you determine when a choice you make is a genuine sacrifice.

Sacrifice is personal. God's request for a sacrifice and your corresponding response is a very personal experience. It isn't possible for another person to define what constitutes a sacrifice by you. No other person really knows your "heart"—your motives, desires, impulses, and secret longings. No one else understands your emotional investment in what you are considering surrendering, the events and circumstances triggering those connections, and the strength of your faith in that moment. What might appear to be a great sacrifice to others, you may not consider all that difficult. In other cases, what others consider insignificant may create emotional turmoil and spiritual struggles for you.

When we moved to Oregon to become church planters, many women commiserated with my wife about her sacrifice to move so far and risk so much. She accepted their comfort—but it was difficult because she felt no sense of sacrifice in our decision. Our relocation fulfilled her lifelong dream of being appointed by a mission board, moved her closer to her extended family, and allowed her to rear her children in a missionary setting (another long-held desire). Ann was giddy about moving, not depressed over the supposed sacrifice she was making. From an outsider's perspective, moving to Oregon was a sacrifice. From Ann's perspective, it was a joyful fulfillment of her dreams.

In subsequent years, we have been asked to consider ministry assignments requiring relocation from the West Coast. Each time, Ann has said, "I have no interest in leaving the West. But if God asks me to, I will make the sacrifice to move to another part of the country." This probably puzzles some of you who live in other wonderful places! But for us, living on the West Coast is a blessing and moving would be the challenge. Sacrifice is a personal matter. What constitutes a sacrifice is unique to each individual. No one else can define it for you.

Judy, a missionary wife, serves in a remote jungle outpost in South America. When we met her, we were amazed at her faith, her resilience in the face of hardship, and her confidence in God. Given the sacrifices she has made, we were surprised when we learned of an incident when she received a package of goodies from home, only to have her favorite treat stolen and eaten by a villager. She cried out to God, "Father, why did this have to happen? I have given so much, why can't I have this small treat?" She later laughed about it, but the story reveals an important insight into sacrifice. Sometimes, giving up what may seem like a small thing can seem more difficult than moving halfway around the world. What constitutes a sacrifice for you is a personal matter too complex for outside analysis and conclusive judgment by others. You have to discover what sacrifice involves—for you, not for anyone else—and then be willing to make those hard choices.

Sacrifice is proportional. For many years, capital fund-raisers have used the theme Not Equal Gifts, but Equal Sacrifice to challenge people to give to major ministry projects. This theme echoes the biblical pattern of proportional giving. The concept of tithing (giving 10 percent of your resources) is one expression of this pattern. Jesus underscored the important of evaluating our gifts proportionally by affirming the woman who gave two small coins (Luke 21:1–4). She was honored because of the ratio of her gift to her resources, not because of the size of her contribution. Sacrifice is proportional. What constitutes a sacrifice for one person may be pocket change for another. Sorting this out can be complicated when it relates to money and even more difficult in other areas.

Toby is a self-made millionaire. His church was building a new facility and he struggled with how much to give. He could have given the amount needed to build the entire complex. But, he knew that wasn't a wise decision for the overall health of the church. The entire church needed to participate and his gift, while it needed to be a sacrifice for him, also needed to be part of God's larger plan for the rest of the membership to share the load. He struggled with how much to give, finally settling on a significant contribution that drained, but didn't deplete, his considerable resources. Toby determined a sacrifice meant giving enough to alter his standard of living, forsaking personal items or investments he had previously planned to purchase. Making a sacrifice isn't always about giving all you have but it does involve self-limiting, proportional choices prioritizing the needs of others above your own.

Carl and Betty also struggled with making a sacrificial gift to a major ministry project. When they got married, money was tight so they had no honeymoon. They vowed on their twenty-fifth anniversary to have the honeymoon of their dreams—a trip to Australia.

Throughout their marriage, they set aside money every month for their honeymoon account. Some months it was only a few dollars, some much more. Over the years, God blessed them financially and enabled them to fund their dream. All that was left was calling the travel agent.

Then their church asked them to lead a fund-raising campaign for a new campus. As part of the process, they asked God what He wanted them to sacrifice for the project. Their mutually agreed-to answer: give away their trip money. When the story of their gift became known, dozens of other people reevaluated their giving plans and contributed more generously. Today, a beautiful campus stands testimony to their sacrifice, along with the gifts of others who set aside personal desires to obey God and give generously. In this case, while the amount was important, the proportional emotional investment in the honeymoon fund was far more substantial. Giving this money away was sacrificing a dream. It's hard to quantify the proportionality of sacrificing a lifelong dream for the good of others.

Sacrifice involves personal and proportional self-limiting choices with two primary commodities—time and money. Sacrifice can also

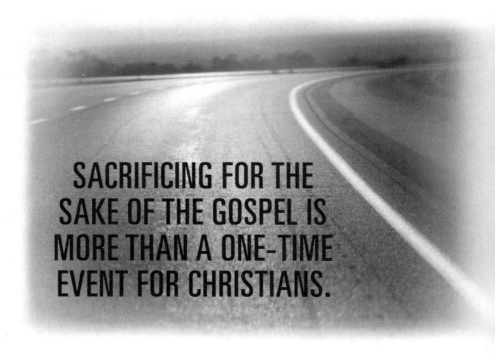

SACRIFICING FOR THE SAKE OF THE GOSPEL IS MORE THAN A ONE-TIME EVENT FOR CHRISTIANS.

involve two other important life issues—relationships and privileges. Considering all four of these as venues for sacrifice will help you understand a more holistic view of this subject. Sacrificing for the sake of the gospel is more than a one-time event for Christians. It's a lifelong pattern revealing a spirit of sacrifice cultivated and enhanced over time. Here are examples of how you can develop this spirit of sacrifice, using four primary commodities (money, time, relationships, and privileges) to advance the gospel.

SACRIFICING YOUR MONEY

Giving money can be one form of sacrifice. A financial sacrifice means giving money or possessions you could have used personally to benefit someone else. All of us can find creative ways to spend all the money we have. Giving away financial resources, to the point it becomes a sacrifice, means making do with less so others can have more. To create the habit or pattern of sacrificial giving to expand the gospel, try these simple steps.

Give more than a tithe. Giving a tithe of your income is the basic standard of Christian stewardship. If you haven't yet established this minimum giving threshold, you aren't ready to progress to sacrificial offerings. The tithe, 10 percent of your gross income, is the basic level of giving expected of every believer. Moving beyond it creates the opportunity to sacrifice by giving optional offerings from resources you might otherwise spend on yourself. You may bristle at that conclusion—believing the tithe is an Old Testament concept not required of New Testament believers. Think again! While the tithe originated in the Old Testament, that doesn't mean it isn't applicable today as a baseline for Christian givers.

Consider how the New Testament (or New Covenant) handles a few other significant Old Testament issues. In the Old Testament, atonement was accomplished by animal sacrifice. In the New Covenant, it's accomplished by a better sacrifice—Jesus (Hebrews 10:1–10). In the Law, adultery was forbidden (Exodus 20:14). Jesus cautioned against even thinking lustful thoughts (Matthew 5:27–30). The Law forbade murder (Exodus 20:13). Jesus outlawed holding bitterness and hatred in your heart (Matthew 5:21–26). Do you see the pattern? The New Covenant supersedes the Old. It replaced the Law, clarified its demands, but didn't diminish its expectations. It amplifies them and makes them more personal. Giving principles aren't exempt from this pattern. New Testament giving (sometimes called grace giving) exceeds the requirement of the Law and challenges us to grow beyond the tithe. Those gifts, usually called offerings, are the opportunity to sacrifice for kingdom advance.

One way to increase the percentage of your income you give away is to raise the percentage incrementally over time. You may only be able to do this in quarter or half percentage point increments each year, but slight progress is still progress. We have followed this pattern for more than 30 years, consistently but slowly increasing the percentage of our income we give away. Now, after many years, we are giving much more than a tithe and enjoying the satisfaction of sacrificing to support ministry projects expressing our passions. This is a slow-but-steady way to build a spirit of sacrifice into your regular giving habits. Through our giving, we are spreading the gospel not only in our community but around the world.

Give alms. American Christians have the benefit of their gifts being tax deductible. While this is a financial blessing we should take advantage of, it shouldn't be the motive for giving to kingdom ministry or people in need. One way to purify your giving motives is to give alms. That out-of-date word describes gifts to the poor, given directly to people in need with no accounting record and no tax benefit.

These gifts remind us to sacrifice to help others, not for the benefits we receive, but because it's the right thing to do. Giving alms might be sending cash to a struggling student, helping a single mother buy groceries, supporting an aging relative with an income supplement, or paying rent for an unemployed friend. These direct cash gifts, given quietly (or anonymously) help you remember the reason you give. They will also make your giving more personal and make your sacrifice more specific. When you give alms, you are giving money you could have spent on yourself to meet a direct, visible need in another person's life.

Give away a prized possession. A greedy spirit can be broken by giving away a prized possession. During my years of pastoral leadership, my churches received many unusual gifts including cars, jewelry, stock funds, and land. Most of these usually came with a story of personal struggle related to obeying God when He asked for something near and dear, along with reports of the subsequent freedom from materialism felt by the donor.

Prior to our engagement, we attended a worship service in which the speaker preached on materialism and a solution to breaking the stronghold of greed: giving away a prized possession. God impressed me to give away my savings account, a small amount by today's standards but representative of a prized possession and a future dream. My savings account was for Ann's engagement ring.

After the service, I told Ann of my impression to give my savings to a fellow college student who was struggling to pay his tuition. She didn't know the money was for her engagement ring. Typical Ann, she told me, "If you're sure God wants you to give the money away, obey Him no matter how bad you think you need to keep it." The next day, I withdrew the entire amount and gave it to a friend.

Something supernatural happened. I felt empowered and freed from the control of money. As a younger Christian, this was a powerful experience. I had obeyed God, breaking the cycle of self-dependence represented by my savings and trusting God to replenish it at His pleasure. Looking back, knowing God resupplied the money and the ring was purchased a few months later, it's easy to forget the real lesson in this story. God was teaching me to sacrifice for Him, trusting He would take care of me. When Ann later learned she had encouraged me to give away her engagement ring money, we had a big laugh. But, more than 30 years later, while we have struggled at times to remember the lesson, we have always come back to what we learned so long ago. When God asks for a sacrifice, He can be trusted to take care of His children who obey Him. Giving away a prized possession is one way to break greed's control and enhance your capacity for sacrifice.

SACRIFICING YOUR TIME

When challenged to greater generosity, Harold told me, "I don't give my money. I give my time." While he was wrong on the first half of his sacrificial equation, he nailed the second part. Christians often must give time they could have spent on personal pursuits to building relationships for the gospel. While it isn't a substitute for obedient monetary giving, reaching out to people with the gospel takes time—another form of sacrifice.

It takes time to build relationships for sharing your faith. Some people are slow to open themselves to the gospel. Serving them, patiently building a relational bridge for the gospel, may take years rather than days. Spending time with unbelievers on their agenda and timetable, rather than pursuing other activities, is a slow-but-steady sacrifice for the gospel. Ann leads a Bible study for women interested in the gospel. Bible study is a loose description. Mostly, they gather to hear Ann teach them the Bible. It took more than a year for the first woman to study the Bible on her own and prepare for the group session. More than a year is a long time! But Ann patiently worked, prayed, encouraged, and supported these women in their embryonic interest in the gospel.

It also takes time to plan, lead, and follow up on outreach activities. Whether it's lunch with a friend or a full-blown evangelism event designed to communicate the gospel to an entire community, it takes time to make, implement, and follow through on a plan.

Deanne wanted to share the gospel with friends on her college campus. She spent weeks building a support team, securing permission for a meeting, arranging a speaker, printing information and promoting the event, extending personal invitations through her circle of influence, praying for God's blessing on the effort, raising money to pay the expenses, and finally, hosting it when it happened. Then, the work really began! She had to follow up with those who participated, troubleshoot misunderstandings that arose among some attendees, organize discipleship groups for the new believers, and assimilate newly discovered seekers into other opportunities for Christian contact. Her dream to share the gospel in a prominent way on her campus turned into a semester-long part-time job.

Living for the gospel, instead of yourself, results in scheduling adjustments and new demands on your time. Sacrificing your time is essential for building relationships, organizing projects, or otherwise investing yourself in activities to share the gospel.

SACRIFICING RELATIONSHIPS

Christians value relationships, and rightly so. People matter more than things and believers should prioritize relationships. Given this priority, is there ever a time to sacrifice relationships to advance the gospel? Surprisingly, the answer is yes. Jesus implied this would be necessary when He promised,

> *And everyone who has left houses, brother or sisters, father or mother, children, or fields because of My name will receive 100 times more and will inherit eternal life* (MATTHEW 19:29).

> *Someone told Him, "Look, Your mother and Your brothers are standing outside, wanting to speak to You." But He replied to the one who told Him, "Who is My mother and who are My brothers?" And stretching out His hand toward His disciples, He said, "Here are My mother and My brothers! For whoever does the will of My Father in heaven, that person is My brother and sister and mother"* (MATTHEW 12:48–50).

While Christians value relationships, relational closeness must sometimes be sacrificed to obey God. One way relational closeness is sacrificed is by moving far from your family. Missionaries serve in distant states or countries. When they do, they forsake the comforts of relational intimacy with extended family. They miss out on graduations, birthday parties, and holiday gatherings. Watching grandchildren leave, moving with their parents to distant locations is one of the most heart-wrenching relational sacrifices made for the gospel. Spiritual maturity is required to leave your family or encourage your family to move away from you for the sake of the gospel. It's a hard sacrifice to give up close family relationships.

Another way relational closeness is sacrificed is choosing to follow Jesus when family members object. Lisa is a committed Christian married to Tony, also a devoted believer. Lisa's parents have consistently objected to her Christian faith. When she married Tony, they told her they had no intention of recognizing their union by attending the wedding or with any contact afterward. For almost ten years, Lisa has made occasional overtures to her parents, but they maintain their rejection of her family because of their faith. Tony has become a successful professional. They have two beautiful children. Yet, Lisa's parents still maintain their distance. While it seems unconscionable, some people must choose between Jesus and a relationship with their family. As painful as it is, the correct choice is Jesus.

SACRIFICING PRIVILEGES

Recently, a simple sacrifice of privilege on an airplane reminded me how significant small acts of kindness can be. My seatmate was a young soldier dressed in military uniform. Just before departure, a passenger came back from first class and said, "Son, this boarding pass has your name on it. Take it and go up to first class. Seat 3A belongs to you. Thanks for serving our country." The soldier tried to decline, but several of us urged him to accept the offer. He did, and my new seatmate was a businessman who sacrificed his right to a first-class seat to express his gratitude for a young man's service to our country.

Some Christians subtly consider certain things, particularly aspects of their relationship with their church to be their rights. One frustrated woman complained when a first-time guest was sitting in her pew. Another person whined, "No one from the church came to visit me in the hospital" (when a deacon made the visit instead of the pastor). A parent of two teenagers demanded to know, "Why doesn't the youth pastor care enough to spend more time with my children?" All these church members had one thing in common—unmet expectations of their right to special treatment from others. While expressions of deference and support by fellow church members or leaders are appreciated, they aren't our rights as believers. When demanding your rights becomes your focus, you have drifted from service into selfishness—motivated by a sense of self-entitlement rather than a spirit of sacrifice.

Christians focused on getting the gospel to others are too busy sacrificing themselves to complain about some real or perceived slight of their so-called rights. On the contrary, they look for ways to make sure the focus stays off them and on those who need the gospel. Kenny told me from his hospital bed, "Thanks for coming, Pastor. But I'm fine. Your time is too precious to spend it checking on me. Go tell somebody about Jesus instead!" Christians like Kenny aren't concerned with their rights or privileges of kingdom or church membership. They prefer the focus be on others. They are more concerned with their responsibilities than their rights, with caring for others rather than demanding their privileges. Christians must consider sacrifice a privilege, rather than considering themselves worthy of special privileges.

THE SECRET SACRIFICIAL CHRISTIANS KNOW

Changing your lifestyle to be more sacrificial may sound onerous and depressing. You may imagine drudgery and emptiness, compounded by loneliness and deprivation. While the process of considering a sacrifice—giving money, investing time, giving up close relationships, or surrendering a privilege—may be difficult, the aftermath is surprisingly satisfying. Jesus promised, "There is no one who has left a house, wife or brothers, parents or children because of the kingdom of God, who will not receive many times more at this time, and eternal life in the age to come" (Luke 18:29–30). Whatever you give up to share the gospel with someone else will come back to you multiplied countless times over in this life and the next.

Paul expressed this in another way when he told the Ephesians, "So then I ask you not to be discouraged over my afflictions on your behalf, for they are your glory" (Ephesians 3:13). He didn't regret his sacrifice for his fellow believers. He relished the opportunity, reminding them his sacrifices were a "glory" for him, and also for the believers at Ephesus.

Here's the secret sacrificial Christians know: the rewards of sacrificing for the gospel far exceed any loss involved. Christians aren't depressed monks wandering around in sackcloth and ashes. We are happy, content, joyful, willing servants who have discovered a profound spiritual secret. Jesus was right! When you give your life away, you really find it. "Anyone finding his life will lose it, and anyone losing his life because of Me will find it" (Matthew 10:39). When you give generously, your supply will be replenished beyond your capacity to contain it. "Give, and it will be given to you; a good measure—pressed down, shaken together, and running over—will be poured into your lap" (Luke 6:38). Even when you sacrifice relational closeness, you are rewarded with substitute relationships galore. "I assure you: There is no one who has left a house, wife or brothers, parents or children because of the kingdom of God, who will not receive many times more at this time, and eternal life in the age to come" (Luke 18:29–30).

Sacrifice isn't spiritual castor oil. Sacrifice is the sweet nectar of spiritual obedience. As a Christian, cultivate a spirit of sacrifice. Choose to make consistent choices to put the needs of others, particularly unbelievers, ahead of your needs. Doing this is a privilege as you follow the example of Jesus, emptying ourselves so others can hear the gospel, receive salvation, and enjoy eternal life in heaven. Whatever that costs, it's worth it!

LIFE HAPPENS—
UNSCRIPTED, BUT AMAZING

CHAPTER 10

DOING MORE
THAN YOU
EVER IMAGINED

L EADERS SOMETIMES MAKE audacious statements and
then lead people to fulfill them. Leaders turn their convictions
about what must happen and their vision about what can
happen into what does happen. When they do, the world is changed,
often dramatically, with results echoing to subsequent generations. In
the 1960s two American leaders made bold pronouncements, which
they were later instrumental in fulfilling. Their words—simple,
direct, challenging—changed our world.

Speaking to a special joint session of Congress on May 25,
1961, President John F. Kennedy said, "I believe that this nation
should commit itself to achieving the goal, before this decade is out,
of landing a man on the moon and returning him safely to the earth.
No single space project in this period will be more impressive to
mankind, or more important for the long-range exploration of space;
and none will be so difficult or expensive to accomplish." By the end
of the decade, despite Kennedy's tragic assassination, Neil Armstrong

stepped on the lunar surface with his triumphant statement, "That's one small step for man; one giant leap for mankind." Kennedy's visionary leadership galvanized a nation, accelerated space exploration, and perhaps most importantly, fueled scientific and technological growth that changed America forever. One brief statement by a brash, young President called a country to achieve something heretofore considered impossible—landing a man on the moon and returning him safely to earth. The results left a multigenerational impact of technological advance still reverberating today.

Another leader at the end of the same decade made a similar prediction, also with long-lasting results. When voiced, it didn't carry the weight of a pronouncement by a US President. It seemed braggadocian, even frivolous. Yet, the economic and cultural changes ultimately produced by this prediction and its aftermath also changed American culture. Speaking to the Miami Touchdown Club three days before Super Bowl III, New York Jets quarterback Joe Namath said, "We're gonna win the game. I guarantee it." The Jets, from the upstart American Football League, did win, setting in motion a series of events resulting in the creation of the modern National Football League. The NFL is a multibillion-dollar enterprise that has profoundly shaped American culture. Not only is the league itself worth billions, its impact has been felt in creating or impacting other multibillion dollar industries—like the growth of college football, the promotion of NFL players as marketing icons, and even the creation of fantasy football (played by millions of people every year). Two statements, by two very different leaders more than 50 years ago, set in motion events that have changed and continue to change our world.

During His lifetime, Jesus made several world-changing statements. He often challenged His followers—including you—to accomplish more than they previously thought possible. One statement by Jesus, however, towers above the others. It seems impossible to fulfill, yet demands our serious attention to discover how to live it out. Jesus said:

I assure you: The one who believes in Me will also do the works that I do. And he will do even greater works than these, because

I am going to the Father. Whatever you ask in My name, I will do it so that the Father may be glorified in the Son. If you ask Me anything in My name, I will do it. If you love Me, you will keep My commands. And I will ask the Father, and He will give you another Counselor to be with you forever (JOHN 14:12–16).

Jesus said His followers would do "the works that I do" and (astoundingly) "greater works than these." Unbelievable! Jesus called you, an everyday Christian, to do greater works than He accomplished. Quite bluntly, that doesn't seem possible. As you consider impacting your world by more intentionally sharing the gospel, the challenge can seem daunting, even impossible. Based on Jesus' bold statement, supernaturally changing your world may seem difficult, but it's still possible.

Jesus changed lives. He healed the sick, fed the hungry, and clothed the naked. He confronted the corrupt, battled Satan, and overcame demons. Jesus even raised the dead! The Lord who accomplished so much told you to imitate Him and, beyond that, do even "greater works than these." It's easy to dismiss these claims as a charismatic leader's hyperbole. But this is Jesus speaking. His words are a mandate, not the aimless meanderings of a leader venting superfluous ideas to titillate His hearers. Discovering what Jesus meant, and how to accomplish the greater works He mentions, is essential for fulfilling these important directives.

SEARCHING FOR ANSWERS

What did Jesus mean by greater works? More importantly, how is this possible? How can we, fallible humans, do greater works than Jesus or his first-century followers? Searching for solutions leads to several possible—though inadequate—answers to these questions. First, one possible reason we can do greater works is we have a greater opportunity than existed during Jesus' lifetime. There are more people alive at this moment in history, whenever you are reading this, than ever before. Jesus changes lives and there are more lives that can be changed today than any time in history. We can do greater works because we can reach many more people with the message of salvation than could be reached during Jesus' time on earth.

Second, greater works are possible because there are greater needs, and more people in need, than in any previous generation. Family dysfunction, frequent divorce, and children in crisis create cultural chaos. Wars, genocide, terrorism, and nuclear threat make our world a violent, destructive place. Prejudice and gender bias, particularly among religions that foment discord and depend on oppression to maintain their influence contribute to the turmoil many people experience daily. While many of these same problems existed in the first century, the scope of their destructive influence is much greater today.

Third, greater works are possible because there are better tools for ministry currently available than at any previous time in history. Innovations in communication and transportation are particularly helpful in getting the gospel to more people in less time. Television, radio, cell phones, computers, and various resources connected to and through the Internet have made formerly isolated people groups more accessible. The international airline network, coupled with other forms of comparatively inexpensive transportation, make it possible to go almost anywhere from almost anywhere in a relatively short time frame.

Finally, Christians today have a greater foundation of ministry expertise than ever before, making possible greater works built on past successes. The church has more than 20 centuries of experience, a significant track record of effectiveness (as well as mistakes we have also learned from). Many problems have been addressed and solved. This accumulated wisdom, for those who are willing to study history and learn from it, makes doing ministry more efficient and effective as we draw on the amassed record of kingdom experiences.

These external factors may be part of what Jesus meant when He said we would do greater works. But while they postulate some possibilities, do they account for the means to do what Jesus said?

No, they don't.

The problem with these suggestions is they are only true for this generation and only for some believers in some locations. They aren't true for all believers in all places for all time. There must, therefore, be other ways and means for us to do greater works. Those resources had to be available immediately after Jesus' ascension and still available today. They must be accessible to all believers,

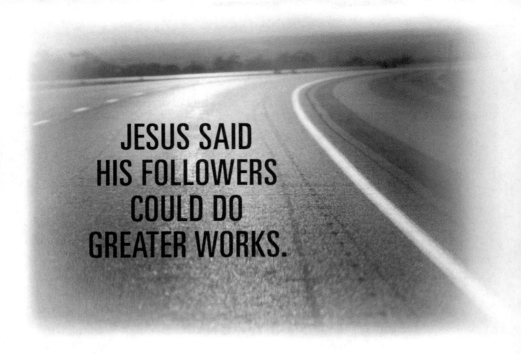

JESUS SAID HIS FOLLOWERS COULD DO GREATER WORKS.

everywhere, and for all believers for all time. Determining what those resources are seems mysterious, until you consider the obvious. In the same discourse, Jesus not only told us to do greater works but He also explained how to do them.

Jesus' instructions for accomplishing greater works are an essential foundation for any Christian in any generation who wants to make an eternal impact on others. Taking seriously Jesus' instructions and learning to apply His insights in contemporary life is the challenge. We simply can't ignore what Jesus said. We must agree to His mandate and use His methodology to fulfill it. When we do, our lives will come alive with the supernatural results we long to achieve.

ACTING ON THE AUTHORITY OF JESUS

The first resource for doing greater works is ministering with Jesus' authority and communicating an authoritative message about Him. Jesus said His followers could do greater works because "I am going to the Father" (John 14:12). Jesus has fulfilled that promise. He ascended to heaven (Acts 1:9–11) and currently resides there in a position of authority. Paul described God's role in the ascension by reporting:

He [God] demonstrated this power in the Messiah by raising Him from the dead and seating Him at His right hand in the heavens—far above every ruler and authority, power and dominion, and every title given, not only in this age but also in the one to come. And He put everything under His feet and appointed Him as head over everything for the church, which is His body, the fulfillment of the One who fills all things in every way (EPHESIANS 1:20–23).

Jesus is now seated at the right hand of God. In a monarchial government, the place of honor and power is on the right side of the ruler. God is the Sovereign of the universe. Jesus is seated at His right hand, a position symbolizing His authority and power. The message of the gospel centers on Jesus—His life, death, resurrection, and His ascension and exaltation. When you share the message of Jesus, what aspect do you emphasize? Evangelists often focus on Jesus' life and death. While that's always appropriate, it's not enough. Ending the story with the death of Jesus truncates the gospel, shortchanging who Jesus is and what He has done. Jesus is no longer a lowly Savior meek and mild. He is now a ruling Lord overseeing His eternal domain.

Christians serve and share the resurrected, ascended Jesus. We tell the story of a powerful Savior and exalted Lord who changes lives. The Resurrection is the distinctive feature of Christianity (1 Corinthians 15:13–14); the Ascension its culmination. The Resurrection demonstrates Jesus' ultimate power over all forces, including death. It validates His ability to change lives. Preaching, teaching, or conversing about Jesus' resurrection seems foolish to modern hearers (1 Corinthians 1:22–23). Nonetheless, Christians have no more powerful message than the story of the resurrected Christ. We tell the story, trusting the ascended Jesus who empowers us to transform those who believe in Him.

Christians speak about the Resurrection and trust the message itself to change lives. We lack the power to raise the dead. Jesus, though, has that power. When we speak of His resurrection and facilitate people experiencing its life-giving power, we have a hand in raising the spiritually dead. Our role is to speak confidently of the Resurrection, trusting the message to transform lives because of its inherent power. As a believer, you have the unique privilege of speaking for a King—with His authority backing your words. Christians can do greater works because of the power of their message and the One who empowers it.

PRAYING IN JESUS' NAME

A second resource for doing greater works is prayer. After predicting His ascension, Jesus said, "Whatever you ask in My name, I will do it so that the Father may be glorified in the Son. If you ask Me anything in My name, I will do it" (John 14:13–14). Praying "in Jesus' name" is more than a habit, a Christian mantra added to the end of every prayer like a stamp assuring it will be delivered to God and promptly answered in the affirmative. When we pray in Jesus' name, we are praying in His authority—like we are praying in His stead or in His place.

Names, in their appropriate context, carry considerable weight. For example, in a company, when a person says, "The president wants this project done," most employees will pick up the pace. Increased productivity isn't achieved because of the person delivering the message. It results from the authority of the person in whose name the message was delivered. When you pray, you speak with the authority (in the name) of Jesus. God hears your prayers, not because of your authority as the one asking, but because of the One in whose name you are praying. When you pray in Jesus' name, you pray in His authority, not your own.

Jesus promises God hears and answers every prayer offered in His name that "the Father may be glorified in the Son." This doesn't mean every prayer is answered yes. Sometimes, God answers with a resounding no, and other times with a distinct not now. God answers prayers to bring Him glory, not satisfy your whims. You err when you assume God hasn't answered your prayers because things don't turn out like you prayed. When you pray, ask boldly. Then have the humility to receive whatever answer God provides. Praying "in Jesus' name" isn't about getting your way, it's about praying for what ultimately brings glory to God.

Christians must learn to ask for things appropriate to using the name of Jesus. If a millionaire told you to withdraw any amount of funds from his account, and granted the authority for it to happen, would you ask for a paltry sum? Probably not. You would ask for an amount in line with the resources available, the authority of the person guaranteeing your request, and your perceived needs. Your request would be fitting of the person in whose name you are making it. We must learn to pray requests worthy of being asked in Jesus' name.

As a young adult, a Bible teacher who focused on prayer had a profound impact on me. Don Miller was intense, passionate, and practical. While teaching a prayer seminar, he asked, "What are you praying for that seems impossible?" That was easy. I was asking God for $500 to pay for college the following semester. It was a huge amount. I wondered if God even had that much money! Then Miller thundered, "I am praying for God to reveal the cure for all cancer in my lifetime." Suddenly, my tiny amount faltered in comparison. All cancer in his lifetime? Wow! Don Miller understood the power of praying in Jesus' name, requesting something worthy of being asked in the name of the Lord of the universe. Several years later, when I was medically cured of thyroid cancer, I remembered that prayer conference. When I arrive in heaven, I hope to learn if my healing was in response to Don Miller's faith-filled praying.

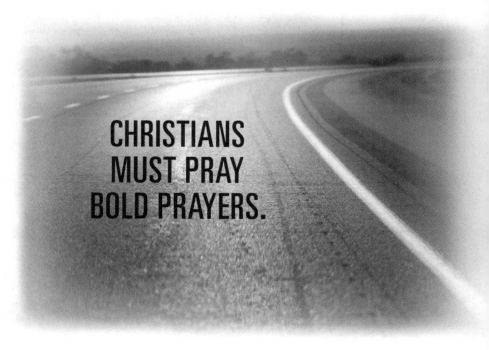

CHRISTIANS
MUST PRAY
BOLD PRAYERS.

Christians must pray bold prayers—asking for what seems impossible and trusting God to do "above and beyond all that we ask or think" (Ephesians 3:20). We ask for people to be saved—the greatest miracle possible today. Further, we ask for opportunities to share the gospel, for insight in sharing the gospel, and for the gospel to spread rapidly (see chap. 2). These seem like impossibilities. God specializes in doing what we can't do, and beyond that, doing more than we even imagine. Ask God boldly, in Jesus' name, prayers worthy of being voiced in the place of someone of such high position. Prayer offered in Jesus' name is a primary means of doing greater works today.

OBEYING GOD'S WORD

A third resource for doing greater works is obeying God's Word. This is the simple, but profound process of aligning your life with Truth revealed in the Bible and helping others do the same. Jesus said, "If you love Me, you will keep My commandments" (John 14:15). He later added: "The one who has My commands and keeps them is the one who loves Me. And the one who loves Me will be loved by My Father. I also will love him and will reveal Myself to him" (John 14:21).

Jesus equated loving Him with obeying Him. Talk is cheap. Actions really do speak louder than words. If you love Jesus, it will be revealed in your actions—not in your declamations of allegiance or affection. Jesus made a remarkable promise to Christians who love and obey Him. He said he would love us and reveal Himself to us. A key phrase to experiencing greater works is the final phrase. Jesus promised to reveal Himself in believers who obey His Word.

When you obey the Bible, Jesus produces His character in you and accomplishes His works through you. This is how He reveals Himself in and through us—life transformation! These are the miraculous changes producing a new quality of life resulting from obeying God's Word. When you teach others to obey the Bible, they experience this same process. Transformation occurs. People are changed as they align themselves with Truth. The greater work of changing lives is facilitated by teaching people the Bible and helping them obey what they learn.

Greg had been a Christian for a few years, but lived much like he did before his conversion. Then he started reading the Bible every

day. He joined a men's group to study the Bible and be held accountable for applying insights as he learned them. Life change started
immediately. Old habits became less controlling. New patterns were
established. Friends and family noticed the changes and were
amazed. Greg was becoming a new person right before their eyes.
Conversion changes you instantly, producing a new birth. Regular
intake of and obedience to God's Word changes you incrementally,
producing a new lifestyle. The Bible is the key ingredient to shaping
your behavior over a lifetime of continuing sanctification.

Christians are powerless to transform others. But our message, the gospel, changes lives by leading a person to conversion.
Our continued work of discipling—teaching a person to align
his or her behavior with God's Word—continues the life change
process. Both of these are greater works—producing the greatest
work, a new person. As people believe the Truth and alter their
behavior accordingly, miraculous change happens and the greatest
work possible—a person saved and sanctified until a new lifestyle
emerges—is accomplished.

ACCESSING THE HOLY SPIRIT'S POWER

A final resource for doing greater works is ministering in the power
of the Holy Spirit. Jesus promised, "I will ask the Father, and He will
give you another Counselor to be with you forever" (John 14:16). A
more thorough discussion of accessing the Holy Spirit's power has
already been provided (see chap. 4). In the context of doing greater
works, however, it's important to again acknowledge our impotence
and inability to produce power for spiritual ministry.

Jesus promised a Helper (also can be translated a Counselor,
Comforter, or Companion) as the Source of spiritual power to
accomplish greater works (John 14:16). The perpetual temptation
is to trust your wisdom, power, insight, authority, or money to for
spiritual success. While your resources are part of the equation,
they are never sufficient to accomplish miraculous results. The
disciples once provided two fish and five loaves (their resources), but
divine power was necessary to feed a multitude (Matthew 14:17).
Proverbs 21:31 says, "A horse is prepared for the day of battle, but
victory comes from the Lord." In short, saddle your horse with every
resource possible—but trust none of them. Prepare yourself in every

way to share the gospel with others, but don't trust your preparation. Trust the Holy Spirit's power to carry you along.

While you must do your part using the resources at hand, don't overestimate your contribution or depend on yourself for supernatural results. The power of the Spirit is essential for doing the greater works Jesus demands. When you apply the insights outlined earlier about the Holy Spirit (again, see chap. 4), you will experience the supernatural power you need for sharing the gospel as life happens.

YOU REALLY CAN DO IT

God has called you to join his mission of getting the gospel to as many people as possible—starting with the people you see every day. If you have read this far, you must be serious about making the lifestyle changes necessary to share the gospel more effectively. Perhaps you are starting at square one, just launching out on the adventure of being less self-centered and more focused on getting the gospel to others. Or, you may be well down the road and found this book to be more encouraging than corrective. No matter where you are on the continuum, God wants to expand your view of His world and your role of communicating the gospel to people in it.

What should you do now? First, do something differently because you have read this book. Don't just read it for spiritual or intellectual stimulation, put it on a shelf, and forget it. Choose a few of the insights and suggestions you have gleaned and put them into practice. Don't make the mistake, however, of trying to do everything you have read all at once. Select some key insights from the book most applicable in your setting and get busy doing those few things. Then later, make additional changes as you continue to develop a better understanding of what it means to share the gospel on the go, as life happens around you.

Second, make purposeful changes to implement new ideas you have discovered. Getting disengaged from other activities so you can devote more time to relationships with unbelievers is a process. Be intentional, but not abrupt in making these changes. Recognize real change takes time to implement. Becoming a more evangelistic Christian is a process of continuing adjustments leading to new patterns, not an overnight shift creating instant success. Be patient, but purposeful, in shaping a new lifestyle.

Third, deepen your dependence on God and trust Him to work through you to advance the gospel. You probably feel a sense of responsibility both for sharing the gospel in your circle of influence and for getting the gospel to all the nations. This weight is a healthy burden and a sobering spiritual reality. Don't forget, however, the ultimate power for accomplishing these goals is divine. God the Spirit is at work through you to communicate the message of God the Son and call unbelievers into a relationship with God the Father. The responsibility to deliver the gospel message is yours, but the power to fulfill the responsibility comes from God. Trust Him, not your own strength, to get the job done.

Finally, attempt the impossible and trust God for the improbable. You may think it unlikely some people in your community, company, or circle of friends will ever become Christians. You don't sense much interest in the gospel. You doubt your capacity to communicate effectively. You wonder if anything you can do will really make a difference. Stop confusing your lack of faith with God's lack of power. Do your part and trust God to do His. Our loving God, who cared enough for unredeemed people to send Jesus to die for them, wants people to be saved and follow Him much more than you do! So get busy, no matter how unlikely it seems you will have any progress, much less success. As you pray, witness, serve, and communicate the gospel, God will do His part.

Life is unscripted. It's an adventure. God is searching for believers who will join Him in reaching out to their neighbors and the nations. Are you ready for God to use you to change the eternal destiny of your friends and family? Are you ready to do more than you have ever imagined helping people come to know Jesus? If so, God is ready to use you to do greater works—supernatural works of transforming people into fully devoted followers of Jesus. Now get moving!

APPENDIX:

APPLICATION OPTIONS

T HROUGHOUT THIS BOOK, applications and steps of action have been identified. But summarizing some of those key concepts in an easy-to-reference way may help you get started putting what you have learned into action. If so, copy these pages and stick them on the refrigerator or your bathroom mirror as a daily reminder of changes you are making. Better yet, use this list to give you some fresh ideas and create your own list based on all you have read.

- Pray.
- Pray you will join God's harvest in a fresh way.
- Pray for other believers to join you working in the harvest.
- Pray for alertness to more opportunities to witness.
- Pray for spiritual discipline to keep your witness focused on Jesus.
- Pray for wisdom to witness effectively—no matter the situation you may face.
- Pray for boldness to talk about Jesus.
- Pray for the gospel to spread rapidly through your community.
- Pray for friends and family, by name, to be saved.

STUDY THE GOSPEL

- Read your church's doctrinal statement to clarify what you believe about the gospel.
- Ask your pastor to recommend a doctrinal study or good book on the gospel.
- Complete a practical course on how to share the gospel conversationally.
- Identify theological questions you have about the gospel and resolve them with a pastor or other spiritual mentor.
- Identify relational tension you feel when sharing the gospel and discuss it with a pastor or other spiritual mentor.

EXPERIENCE THE HOLY SPIRIT

- Read your church's doctrinal statement to clarify what you believe about the Holy Spirit.
- Ask your pastor to recommend a doctrinal study or a good book on the Holy Spirit.
- Seek, through prayer on a daily basis, the filling of the Holy Spirit for ministry to others, including sharing the gospel.
- Confess known sin and stop sinful behavior that may be an impediment to the Spirit's flow through you.
- Initiate spiritual disciplines (daily Bible reading, prayer, worship attendance, Scripture memory, fasting, etc.) that accentuate your sensitivity to the Spirit.

BUILD RELATIONSHIPS

- Make a list of friends, family, and people in your circle of influence who you want to be more sensitive to regarding their spiritual condition and interest.
- If you do not have many unsaved friends, make a list of acquaintances you could befriend in more intentional ways.
- Take an acquaintance to lunch, coffee, a sporting event, or a concert, any mutually enjoyable activity that would provide an opportunity for building a relationship leading to a conversation about the gospel.
- Adjust your attitude toward unbelievers who may behave

in unseemly ways you find offensive. Choose to love people and ignore behavior!

- If you are not connected to non-Christian communities, join a club or a group with which you share a common interest. Make friends!

DETERMINE TO CHANGE

- Overcome your reticence to share a verbal witness about Jesus and reject any definition of witnessing that doesn't include communicating the gospel.
- Overcome any embarrassment you have about the gospel because of the behavior of other Christians or negative prejudice in your community toward Christianity.
- Overcome religious barriers well-meaning Christians have erected that prevent you from connecting the gospel with your community.
- Overcome cultural barriers and other prejudices that prevent you from sharing the gospel with all people in your circle of influence.
- Overcome limitations on evangelistic methods you may have allowed to limit your creativity in communicating the gospel.

ADJUST YOUR LIFESTYLE

- Identify frivolous activities on which you are wasting time. Eliminate them from your schedule and devote more time to evangelistic endeavors.
- Identify ways you are wasting money that could be used or kingdom purposes. Redirect those funds to evangelistic activities.
- Identify a sacrifice you are willing to make so someone can hear the gospel—and make it today!

OTHER BOOKS ON
MISSIONAL

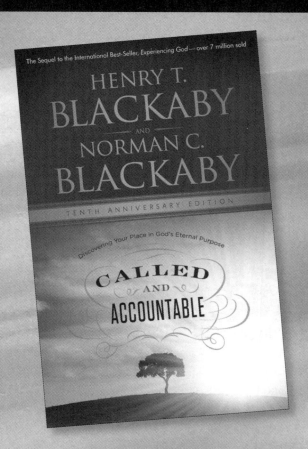

Called and Accountable
Discovering Your Place in God's Eternal Purpose,
Tenth Anniversary Edition
Henry T. Blackaby and
Norman C. Blackaby
ISBN-13: 978-1-59669-352-4
$14.99

LIVING

Compelled
Living the Mission of God
Ed Stetzer and
Philip Nation
ISBN-13: 978-1-59669-351-7
$14.99

Live Sent
You Are a Letter
Jason C. Dukes
ISBN-13: 978-1-59669-315-9
$14.99

New Hope® Publishers is a division of WMU®, an international organization that challenges Christian believers to understand and be radically involved in God's mission. For more information about WMU, go to wmu.com. More information about New Hope books may be found at NewHopeDigital.com. New Hope books may be purchased at your local bookstore.

Use the QR reader on your
smartphone to visit us online at
NewHopeDigital.com

If you've been blessed by this book, we would like to hear your story. The publisher and author welcome your comments and suggestions at: newhopereader@wmu.org.